The hm Learning and Study Skills Program

Student Text Level 2

Fourth Edition

Edited by Judy Tilton Brunner and Matthew S. Hudson, EdD

ROWMAN & LITTLEFIELD EDUCATION
A Division of Rowman & Littlefield
Lanham • Boulder • New York • Toronto • Plymouth, UK

Published by Rowman & Littlefield Education
A division of Rowman & Littlefield
4501 Forbes Boulevard, Suite 200, Lanham, Maryland 20706
www.rowman.com

10 Thornbury Road, Plymouth PL6 7PP, United Kingdom

British Library Cataloguing in Publication Information Available

Library of Congress Cataloging-in-Publication Data
The HM learning and study skills program : level 2. Student text / edited by Judy
Brunner and Matthew Hudson. —4th edition.
     pages cm
  Includes bibliographical references and index.
  ISBN 978-1-4758-0377-8 (pbk. : alk. paper)—ISBN 978-1-4758-0378-5 (electronic)
  1. Study skills—Problems, exercises, etc. I. Brunner, Judy Tilton, 1952– II. Hudson,
Matthew, 1978–
  LB1049.H57 2014
  371.30281—dc23   2013030523

∞™ The paper used in this publication meets the minimum requirements of American
National Standard for Information Sciences—Permanence of Paper for Printed Library
Materials, ANSI/NISO Z39.48-1992.

Printed in the United States of America

CONTENTS

INTRODUCTION TO THE hm LEARNING AND STUDY SKILLS PROGRAM: LEVEL II

LET'S GET STARTED: WHAT ARE LEARNING AND STUDY SKILLS?

Learning and study skills are skills for life. They are methods, ways of doing things, that can help make learning easier for you. They can also help you to get more work done and to learn more in a given period of time. There are skills involved in much of what we do in life, such as playing a musical instrument, shooting a jump shot, sewing a piece of clothing, tuning an engine, baking a cake, or dancing. If you master the skills from this learning module, you will be able to learn more efficiently and effectively in any learning situation.

You must remember, *learning and study skills* are not substitutes for hard work. However, using these skills will help you gain more from the effort and time you devote to learning, particularly to schoolwork.

Many of you are probably already using at least some *learning and studying skills*. This program can help you to learn other skills that will let you use your time and energy even more effectively.

Learning and study skills are methods for acquiring knowledge, understanding, and competence. In the literal sense, *learning and study skills* involve specific, observable behaviors that can be described and measured. For example:

- Can you attend to a set of directions and follow them accurately?

- Can you plan the use of your study time and follow that schedule?

- Can you take useful notes from an oral presentation?

- Can you read a section of text and identify the main ideas and important details?

Study skills are processes for learning. They are designed to help you organize and direct the effort you invest in learning, and their use results in more effective and efficient learning. When you master a skill for learning, you are learning more than just a technique. You are learning a way of solving learning problems, a method of approach and follow-through that can be used in any relevant context. You are also learning more about how to learn effectively.

What do you know about studying?

STUDY SKILLS PRE-TEST

Read each statement carefully. Answer each one as *true* or *false* based upon your personal knowledge of how to study efficiently. During the discussion of each statement, make notes under each one explaining *why* the answer is *true* or *false*.

T_____ F_____ 1. For most students, the best time to study is immediately after school.

_____

_____

_____

_____

_____

T_____ F_____ 2. When you do not understand what is read, immediately reread the assignment for clarification.

_____

_____

_____

_____

_____

T_____ F_____ 3. Underlining or highlighting text is as effective as taking written notes.

_____

_____

_____

_____

_____

T_____ F_____ 4. Always preview the text features and structure of the text prior to reading an assignment.

_____

_____

_____

_____

_____

T____ F____ 5. Studying is only helpful when you are in the mood to do so.

_____
_____
_____
_____
_____

T____ F____ 6. Studying in bed is seldom beneficial to a productive study session.

_____
_____
_____
_____
_____

T____ F____ 7. If content of the text is challenging, find something easier to read on the same subject.

_____
_____
_____
_____
_____

T____ F____ 8. When taking notes, wait until the end of the section to record the notes.

_____
_____
_____
_____
_____

T____ F____ 9. Listening to background music with a headset helps to eliminate unnecessary distractions.

_____
_____
_____
_____
_____

T_____ F_____ 10. Students should read the author's questions prior to reading a text.

_____

_____

_____

_____

_____

T_____ F_____ 11. Drawing pictures while taking notes is not as helpful as using the words from a text.

_____

_____

_____

_____

_____

T_____ F_____ 12. Doodling and drawing unrelated pictures can help to increase the concentration.

_____

_____

_____

_____

_____

T_____ F_____ 13. For consistency's sake, try to read all texts at the same pace.

_____

_____

_____

_____

_____

T_____ F_____ 14. Studying for an exam should begin from the first day of class.

_____

_____

_____

_____

_____

T____ F____ 15. Flash cards are seldom helpful when memorizing vocabulary words and terms.

_____

_____

_____

_____

_____

T____ F____ 16. A good principle is to study at the same time and the same place each day.

_____

_____

_____

_____

_____

T____ F____ 17. To outline effectively, you do not have to think logically.

_____

_____

_____

_____

_____

T____ F____ 18. When only limited study time is available, learn the vocabulary terms first.

_____

_____

_____

_____

_____

T____ F____ 19. A few minutes after each lecture should be designated for reviewing and organizing notes.

_____

_____

_____

_____

_____

INTRODUCTION

T____ F____ 20. Self-quizzing is a good way to prepare for an exam.

_____

_____

_____

_____

_____

UNIT I
ENVIRONMENT MATTERS

INTRODUCTION

In this unit, you are going to look at how you study, that is, how you do your schoolwork outside of class. Also, you will find suggestions that can help you learn to study more effectively.

STUDY ENVIRONMENT

Your environment is everything that surrounds you. Your *study environment*, then, is what surrounds you when you study.

Exercise I

Directions: Answer the questions below, and you will develop a picture of your *study environment*.

1. Where do you usually study at home? _____

   _____

2. What can you see around you when you are studying? _____

   _____

3. What can you hear around you when you are studying? _____

   _____

4. Where do you keep your supplies (books, paper, pens and pencils, etc.) for studying? _____

   _____

5. If you use a computer at home, where is it? _____

   _____

6. Where do you study at school? _____

    _____

7. Is there anywhere else that you study? If so, describe it. _____

    _____

WHAT IS A GOOD STUDY ENVIRONMENT?

People learn in many different ways. We are all individuals and have our own ways of doing things, our own learning styles. So, what is a good study environment for one person may be different from that of another person. However, there do seem to be some parts of a study environment that are good for most people.

Exercise II

Directions: What parts of a study environment do you think might be good for most people? On the lines below, list what you think are two things that support a good study environment.

A. _____

B. _____

DESCRIPTION OF A GOOD STUDY ENVIRONMENT

A. _____

    _____

    _____

B. _____

    _____

    _____

C. _____

    _____

    _____

D. _____

    _____

    _____

SUGGESTIONS FOR CREATING A GOOD STUDY ENVIRONMENT

A. Choose a place at home for studying where you feel comfortable, and study in that place. If you have your own room, that may be the best place. If not, choose a place to study where you will be interrupted by other people as little as possible. Tell your family members about your location for studying, and ask them to help you by not interrupting when you are studying.

B. When you study, try to remove things that will distract you. TV, iPods, and video games are very distracting and will take your attention away from what you are trying to learn. So will a window if you sit in front of one. The fewer distractions you can see, the more effective your learning will probably be.

C. Noise is also a powerful distraction. Try to make your study place as quiet as possible. Ask people not to talk to you when you are studying. If you usually study with music on, try working without it for a week. Give yourself a chance to find out if you can learn better without it.

D. Some people can study even if they are surrounded by distractions. But it takes energy to block them out. When you remove these distractions from your study environment, then you can put that energy into learning. That is why most people can study better in an environment with few or no distractions. When you do remove distractions from your study place, it may take a week or so before you feel comfortable without them and can really see the results. So, give your new study environment a week or two, and then see if it helps you to concentrate and learn. Remember: the key question is, does it help me to study better?

E. If it is hard for you to find a place at home where you can study, ask your family to help you. Tell them that you are trying to study and that you need to reduce the distractions around you as much as possible. Ask them to help you create a good study environment for the time you need to do your work.

F. If you cannot create a good study environment at home, find out when your local library is open. Many people find the library a good place to study. Or, maybe you can study early in the morning before others in your home have awakened.

Exercise III

Directions: List at least three changes you can make in your own study environment that might make it a better place for you to learn.

1. _____

2. _____

3. _____

SUMMARY

Your *study environment* is everything that surrounds you when you study. What is in your study environment can have an important effect on your learning.

Be aware of your *study environment*:

1. Choose a place at home to study where you feel comfortable, and study in that place.

2. Try to remove as many distractions as you can from your study environment. A distraction is anything that takes your attention away from your studying.

3. When you are studying, try to use the following methods:

   a. Set goals for how much you want to accomplish during each study session. Try to give yourself an idea of how long each assignment will take.

   b. When you start an assignment, quickly tell yourself what you already know about it. Then ask yourself: What am I trying to learn about this? Answer this question.

   c. When you finish an assignment, go over what you have just learned. Tell yourself about it as if you were telling another person.

   d. Figure out what kinds of studying you do best alone and what you can do well with other people.

   e. Find out when you are most awake and alert. Use that time for studying.

   f. Try to study for 25–45 minutes at a time. Then take a break for 5–15 minutes before you start again. Reward yourself during the break by doing something that you enjoy.

TECHNOLOGY ADAPTATION

- Design a PowerPoint presentation with helpful information related to the studying environment. Share it with the class.

- Use a class blog to share positive suggestions related to a good environment for studying.

- Make an electronic nonlinguistic representation of a good place to study.

UNIT II
LEARNING TO LISTEN

QUESTIONS FOR GOOD LISTENERS

Directions: You are going to be involved in an activity to see how carefully you listen. Your teacher will ask questions and you are to write your answers to each question that your teacher asks in the space provided.

1. _____

2. _____

3. _____

4. _____

5. _____

6. _____

LISTENING IS A SKILL

The average secondary school student spends about 55 percent of each day in school listening. That means that you give more time to listening than to anything else that you do in school.

Most people think of listening as something as natural as walking or eating. They do not think of it as anything you have to work at to do well. But as you have seen in the "Questions for Good Listeners," most of us are not naturally good listeners. Why not? Hearing is a natural ability, but listening is more than just hearing. Listening means directing your attention to what you are hearing and trying to make sense of what you have heard.

Listening is a skill. It is one of the most important learning skills because listening is a part of almost everything else that you do. It seems simple, but it is not. Being a good listener does not come naturally. It requires learning and practice.

NEGATIVE HABITS OF LISTENING

a. *The attention faker.* These individuals look attentive but seldom pay close attention. They may block out the teacher's message and believe they are "listening" just because they are in class.

b. *The detail person.* These students pay so much attention to detail that the big picture is seldom understood. They will find it difficult to summarize information, and may have difficulty separating the important information from the less important information.

c. *The tuned-out listener.* These individuals are unwilling to exert the energy necessary for successful listening. This may be a result of the complexity of content, fatigue, medication, or other physically related factors.

d. *The bored listener.* Boredom is often mentioned as an excuse for not completing assignments or listening in class. When students do not recognize why it is important to learn the new information, their minds often wander and they mentally disengage.

e. *The distracted listener.* Some students are distracted by outside noise, thoughts of social situations, gestures, or the overall demeanor of the teacher.

WHY IS IT HARD TO LISTEN EVEN WHEN YOU ARE INTERESTED?

Generally people talk at about 125 words per minute. However, we think at a speed that is four or five times as fast, 500 words per minute or more. That means that your thoughts move much faster than the words you hear. So, it is not surprising that we often let attention wander away from what another person is saying.

The key to becoming a good listener is to be an active listener and to keep your thoughts directed on listening.

WHAT HELPS?

a. *Come to class prepared to listen.* Have a pep talk about paying attention in class. Think about the importance of the topic, and set a goal of listening carefully throughout the entire class period.

b. *Choose an appropriate note-taking system.* A variety of ways to take notes is available. Many involve a two- or three-column format (see Unit III). Be flexible with the format, and design notes that can easily be used to self-quiz. Remember, you are not taking dictation; rather, you are summarizing and recording the most important details.

c. *Be comfortable—but not too comfortable.* Sitting in an uncomfortable chair is never fun when listening to a lecture or class discussion, but sitting on a couch or easy chair may make it too easy to relax and tune out or doze off.

d. *Understand the instructional objectives.* When students understand *why* it is important to know the information, engagement is easier to maintain.

e. *When your mind wanders, be prepared to reengage.* Mentally debate with the author or teacher or, if taking notes, use the time to review them. Try to stay on topic, and do not let the mind stray from the lesson.

f. *Practice listening.* Students should understand listening is a skill that can be learned and should be practiced. Listening and hearing are not the same thing.

g. *Listen for ideas.* Ideas are usually more interesting than facts. When listening during class, students should pay particular attention to statements that are thought provoking or controversial.

h. *Resist paying attention to distractions.* There are many things that can distract students during class, but self-discipline is necessary for most, especially when the information is complex and complicated. Recognize the distraction, but make a conscious effort to ignore noise and other outside stimulation.

i. *When possible, ask questions of the speaker.* One sure way to remain mentally engaged is to listen closely enough to ask questions for the purpose of elaboration or clarification. Students should remember that if they have a question, there is a high probability others are also perplexed.

j. *Stay positive.* Negativity can be contagious, so students should surround themselves with other individuals that have a positive attitude about learning, the class, and the teacher.

COMMON CAUSES OF LISTENING ERRORS

- Focusing on a single word rather than on an entire question or sentence

- Jumping to a conclusion based upon expectations rather than what is actually said

- Not understanding or paying attention to key words

- Switching the order of words

- Not noticing verb tense or other indications of when something happened

- Feeling overwhelmed by the amount of information presented

- Thinking about something else while trying to look as though listening is occurring

- Rehearsing a verbal response before the speaker has completed the thought

- Hearing what is expected, rather than what is said

- Focusing primarily on points of disagreement

HOW CAN YOU BECOME AN ACTIVE LISTENER?

Being an active listener means both hearing the words that are being spoken and thinking about what those words mean. Below you will find three helpful ways to think about what you are hearing:

1. While you listen, ask yourself questions about what the speaker is saying. Then try to answer your questions. Asking and answering questions in this way can help you make sense of the speaker's message.

   ASK YOURSELF: What is the speaker telling me? Do I understand this? What don't I understand about what I'm hearing? Does this make sense to me?

2. Try to "picture" what you are hearing in your mind's eye. Some people can listen and understand better when they use their imaginations to make mental pictures of what they are hearing.

   ASK YOURSELF: Can I see a "picture" of what I'm hearing in my mind's eye?

   Regularly summarize what the speaker has already said. Remind yourself of what has already been covered.

   ASK YOURSELF: What are the main points of what's already been said?

WHAT ELSE CAN YOU DO TO IMPROVE YOUR LISTENING SKILLS?

- Look at the person who is speaking. Establish eye contact if possible. This will help you to pay better attention to what he or she is saying.

- First listen, then judge. Listen to everything that the speaker has to say before you decide how you feel about it. If you begin to react in the middle of listening, then you may miss what he or she will say next. Try to listen to everything first. Then react to it.

- Take notes if you need to remember what has been said. (Unit III will help you with taking notes.)

Exercise I

Directions: Try to be an active listener while your teacher talks. Then answer the questions below about what you have just heard.

1. What are the main points of what has been said?

2. Did you ask yourself any questions while you were listening? If you did, write the questions on the lines below.

_____

_____

_____

_____

3. Were you able to "picture" anything that you heard in your mind's eye? If you could, briefly describe one "picture" that you "saw" on the lines below.

_____

_____

_____

_____

4. Rate your active listening from 1–9 during the past few minutes on the scale below. Circle the descriptor that you think best describes your listening.

Not Listening at All	Listening at Times	Listening but Not Asking Yourself Any Questions	Listening and Asking Yourself Some Questions	Active Listening
1	2	3 4 5	6 7	8 9

SUMMARY

Listening is a skill. It takes effort and practice to learn how to be a good listener; the key is to be an active listener. Remember, active listening includes the following:

1. Asking questions about what the speaker is saying and trying to answer the questions;

2. Making a mental picture of what is heard;

3. Mentally summarizing what the speaker has already said;

4. Looking at the person who is speaking, and establishing eye contact;

5. Listening first, and judging later;

6. Trying to not evaluate what is heard until the entire message has been shared;

7. Taking notes if the information needs to be remembered;

8. Giving the speaker full attention and concentrating on each word;

9. Facing the person that is speaking;

10. Using nonverbal cues like nodding the head to acknowledge what is said; and

11. Reflecting before speaking.

Good listeners are able to summarize or paraphrase what was said to them previously. They attend to what was said and how it was said. Good listeners understand that inflection, tone, and other paraverbal behaviors all contribute to the speaker's message.

TECHNOLOGY ADAPTATION

- Have students take a listening test from an online source. These tests provide the spoken word over a generic subject and a series of comprehension questions to score the student's ability to listen.

UNIT III
NOTE-TAKING METHODS

WHY TAKE NOTES?

The major difficulty that many students have in taking notes is that they are not really sure what they are trying to accomplish. Some students try to copy down every word. Others may only write down a few facts here and there without including any ideas that explain them.

The purpose of taking notes is to help you learn.

To take useful notes, you need to figure out what is important in what you are reading or hearing. You want to write down only the main ideas and important details. Figuring out what you want to include in your notes and jotting it down will help you learn these ideas and details.

Taking notes also gives you a record of what you need to know for the future. Then you can use your notes to study for tests.

Think of your notes as a road map. What you want to write down as notes are words and phrases that will help you to remember the main ideas and important details of what you have read or heard. Just as a road map leaves out a lot of detail, so can your notes.

Always write your notes in your own words. When you put notes into your own words, you can be sure that you understand what your notes mean. You will also understand them when you come back to them later.

So, taking notes helps you to learn when you first write them down. It also gives you a record that you can use later.

USING ABBREVIATIONS AND SYMBOLS IN NOTE TAKING

One good way to save time while taking notes is to use abbreviations and symbols. Use abbreviations and symbols that are generally accepted.

An abbreviation is several letters taken from a word that are used to stand for that word.

Examples of Abbreviations

word	abbreviation
continued	cont.
United States of America	USA
mathematics	math
government	govt.

A symbol is a letter or marking that is used to stand for a word or words.

Examples of Symbols

word	symbol
with	w
and	+
without	w/o

Exercise I

Directions: Create a symbol or abbreviation for each of the following words.

1. California _____   6. leads to _____

2. equals _____   7. because _____

3. department _____   8. biology _____

4. against _____   9. information_____

5. maximum _____   10. decrease _____

TAKING USEFUL NOTES

Many people prefer to take notes in outline form, either formal or informal. Others prefer mapping. Some people use methods other than these two to take notes. Do you know other ways of taking notes?

Some people learn more than one method for taking notes, for example, outlining and mapping. Then they can use outlining in some situations and mapping in others.

What is most important is that you learn a way of taking notes that makes sense to you. Practice both mapping and outlining for a while. Then use the method of note taking that works best for you as a learner. Or, become skillful at using both of these methods, and use them in different situations.

STRATEGY # 1: MAPPING STRATEGY

Mapping is an alternative note-taking method that can prove extremely useful to students (1) when outlining is not a helpful tool, and (2) in situations where the presentation lacks a clear organization, such as class discussion. It requires less organization than outlining does as a student goes along but results in almost equally well-organized notes. Although it may be used in any context, mapping is particularly helpful for taking notes during unstructured oral presentations.

Steps in the Process

1. Read the assigned section of text, or listen to class discussion.

2. Determine the main idea, and print or write the main idea in the center of a sheet of paper.

3. Write the important, supporting details on lines that are connected to the circle around the main idea.

4. When more information is needed for supporting details, write the subdetails on lines that are connected to the lines of the supporting details.

Benefits of Mapping

- Encourages a deeper understanding of the text

- Active involvement rather than passive memorization of key terms

- Prepares you for independent reading

STRATEGY # 2: CORNELL NOTE-TAKING STRATEGY

The primary purpose of the Cornell Note-Taking Strategy is to provide students with an organized and efficient method of taking notes from a lecture and/or text. This note-taking system provides an easy-to-use study guide.

Steps in the Process

1. Draw a line vertically on the left side of a piece of paper.

2. Write important information from the lecture or text in the column on the right side of the paper.

3. After notes are completed, review the notes and write questions from the content in the margin on the left side of the paper.

4. Cover the right column, exposing only the questions on the left. Self-quiz or work with other students to learn the important concepts.

Benefits

- Provides a systematic method for note taking

- Provides a ready-made study guide for review

- Easy to do

STRATEGY # 3: KNOWLEDGE CHART NOTE-TAKING STRATEGY

The Knowledge Chart Procedure is designed to help you think about what you already know and relate it to what you read from the text or hear in a lecture. This strategy supports understanding of the main idea as well as detailed information.

Steps in the Process

1. Using a piece of paper, divide it vertically into two columns of equal size. The teacher may draw a similar graphic organizer to display to the class.

2. At the top of the column on the left, write "Prior Knowledge." At the top of the column on the right, write "Need to Remember."

3. Prior to reading the assigned text, brainstorm what you already know about the topic and record the information in the column under "Prior Knowledge."

4. After reading the passage, list in the "Need to Remember" column notes from the text. Continue until you have listed several pieces of important information.

5. Using the information from both columns, work individually or in small groups to formulate questions for what there is to learn about the topic.

Benefits

- Sets a specific purpose for reading

- Serves as a study guide

STRATEGY # 4: NOTE CUE CARDS NOTE-TAKING STRATEGY

The Note Cue Cards Strategy is designed to help you identify important information from a text as well as to facilitate discussion of key terms and concepts after reading.

Steps in the Process

1. Review the note cue cards. The purpose of the cards is to help you identify important information.

2. Preview the reading selection, read the cards, and think about how the cards apply to the text.

3. Read the next section of text for the purpose of preparing your own questions, answers, and comment cue cards.

Benefit

- Sets a specific purpose for reading

STRATEGY # 5: "NOW I GET IT" NOTE-TAKING STRATEGY

The primary purpose of the "Now I Get It" Strategy is to provide a method for staying mentally engaged during the reading or listening process. The strategy also encourages you to revisit and rethink the information prior to completing the note-taking task.

Steps in the Process

1. Divide notebook paper vertically with three columns.

2. At the top of the column on the left, write the words "I Do." Over the middle column, write the words "I Don't," and over the column on the right, write the words "Need to Remember."

3. While reading a text or listening to a lecture or class discussion, if something is important and easily understandable, record it in the column on the left.

4. If there are questions about the text, discussion, or lecture, record them in the middle column.

5. After seeking clarification for the information in the middle column, review all notes and record the most important parts of the information in the column titled "Need to Remember."

Benefits

- Promotes active listening

- Provides a ready-made study guide for review

- Includes a first review of the notes before putting them away

STRATEGY # 6: TAKE AND REVISE NOTE-TAKING STRATEGY

The Take and Revise Strategy is designed to encourage you to take notes and review and revise them as necessary. The periodic review helps put the information into your long-term memory.

Steps in the Process

1. Draw a line vertically leaving approximately two-thirds of the page to the right of the line.

2. While reading or listening to discussion or lecture, record relevant information in the column on the right side of the page.

3. Within 24 hours, reread the text for the purpose of clarifying and adding to the notes.

4. Review the notes, and make additions or deletions.

5. Use the column on the left to write a brief summary of the information in the other column.

6. At the bottom of each page, write possible test questions related to the content.

Benefits

- Encourages periodic review of notes

- Encourages active reading or listening

- Serves as a study guide

STRATEGY # 7: TEXT STRUCTURE NOTE-TAKING STRATEGY

Using Text Structure Strategy helps you understand how to use features within a text to facilitate understanding and recall of information. While narrative texts usually have a consistent structure, a nonfiction text may have more variety in terms of format.

Steps in the Process

1. Remember that authors use the structure of a text to facilitate understanding. If you do not understand the significance of these features or how to use them advantageously, you may have difficulty focusing, monitoring, and understanding written material.

2. Divide notebook paper into three equal vertical columns. Write "Text Structure" at the top of the column on the left, and write "Example" at the top of the middle column. Write "How This Helps" at the top of the column on the right side of the paper.

3. Complete the organizer by locating the specific support, giving an example of the support, and explaining how the support helps with comprehension. Sample supports include, but are not limited to the following:

    *   Chapter title

    *   Headings

    *   Subheadings

    *   Photos

    *   Bold print

    *   Italics

    *   Diagrams

    *   Graphic organizers

    *   Author questions

    *   Key vocabulary

Benefits

*   Helps you understand the significance of a variety of features on a printed page

*   Facilitates better preparation for reading difficult text as an independent reader

TEXT I

As a result of the Eighteenth Amendment to the Constitution, Prohibition went into effect in all parts of the United States on January 20, 1920. This amendment made the manufacture and use of alcohol illegal, unless it was for medical, industrial, or religious purposes. The Volstead Act was passed by Congress to make it possible for the government to enforce Prohibition. It set up an agency of 1,500 agents who tried to make sure the law was obeyed. However, during the next 13 years, the law did not stop many people from drinking alcoholic beverages. Instead, it led to the creation of a large business for criminals who illegally made liquor and sold it in bars called "speakeas-ies" or by the bottle. Some people made their own liquor, often called "moonshine" or "bathtub gin" at home. The Eighteenth Amendment was finally repealed in 1933. The era of Prohibition was over.

TEXT II

Iron is the most used metal. Nearly 600 million tons of iron are produced throughout the world every year. It is the least costly and most versatile metallic building material. There are few places where metals other than iron must be used.

The purest form of iron in common use is wrought iron. This iron is made by the refining of iron ore. Wrought iron contains carbon and small amounts of other elements as impurities. Its properties are such that its range of use is very limited. Most iron is changed into steel in a second refining step in which some of the carbon is removed. Steel is an alloy—a mixture of iron with other elements.

The properties of iron and its alloy, steel, change greatly with carbon content. Pure iron, which has been made for laboratory use, is silvery white, fairly soft, and magnetic. Wrought iron, containing a little carbon, is much harder, but it can still be worked and hammered easily. Steel varies in its properties from "soft steel" with little carbon content, to tougher and stronger steel with greater amounts of carbon.

Aluminum is the metal next in importance to iron. Almost 2 million tons of aluminum are produced through-out the world each year. An important and useful property of aluminum is its low density, about one-third that of iron. In addition, aluminum is a good conductor of electricity, making it suitable for electricity transmission lines.

Copper is the third most important metal, in terms of tons produced. World production totals about 7.1 mil-lion tons a year. Small amounts of copper are used to make alloys like brass and bronze. Most of the copper pro-duced is used in electrical equipment because it is the best conductor among the common metals.

Only two other metals are used in any significant amounts. The yearly world production of zinc is just over 5.5 million tons. Zinc is used mainly in the protection of steel against rusting. Yearly world production of lead is almost 4 million tons.

TEXT III

During the nineteenth century, women in America had very few rights. All children were considered to be the property of their fathers. When a woman married, she once again belonged to a man; this time she belonged to her husband. The husband became the legal owner of all her property and earnings. Also, women were not allowed to vote or hold public office. Generally, women were considered inferior to men and, thus, not deserving of rights. It was not until the twentieth century that women began to win these rights in most states.

TEXT IV

The air over many cities is polluted. It contains substances released from cars and trucks, industrial smokestacks, and houses and other buildings. As it contains some poisonous materials, polluted air is harmful to health as well as unpleasant to breathe. It can make people cough, choke, cry, and even faint. More seriously, it can also cause respiratory infections, lung cancer, allergies, and several other diseases. Polluted air also hurts plants and reduces the yields of agricultural crops.

TEXT V

Wildlife refuges are areas where wild animals and the environment in which they live are protected from people. Either no hunting at all is allowed, or the amount of hunting is carefully controlled. Most wildlife refuges are owned by the local, state, or federal governments. People are not allowed to live in these areas or use the land for any purpose that would be harmful to the animals. Efforts are made to preserve the land as it is naturally. Also, winter feeding for the animals is provided in some refuges.

SUMMARY

The strategies within this unit support student understanding and comprehension of text. However, most are also suitable for taking notes during a class lecture or discussion, or while viewing a multimedia presentation.

Far too many students fail to make the connection between taking notes and *learning*. Rather, they believe the note taking is a result in and of itself, rather than a tool for future knowledge. Make the connection. You will be glad you did.

Remember the following note-taking tips:

1. To take good notes, figure out what the important ideas and details are in what is being read or heard. Figuring out what these important ideas and details are and then writing them down will help them be learned.

2. Review notes periodically, remembering that a daily review is the most effective way to transmit the information into one's long-term memory.

3. Think of notes as a *map*. Write down only the main ideas and important details. Also, be sure to write notes in your own words.

4. Drawing pictures, symbols, and nonlinguistic representations are useful when taking notes. They support visualization of information.

5. There are a number of ways to "map" information from a text. One of the more common maps is illustrated below.

6. Use abbreviations and symbols as much as possible when taking notes. The more abbreviations and symbols are used, the less writing has to be done, and the more time remaining for reading and listening.

7. Paraphrasing and summarizing when taking notes is a good way to be mentally active while taking notes.

8. Just try to get the main ideas and important, supporting details down on paper.

9. Try to spend 80–90 percent of the time reading or listening, and only 10–20 percent of the time writing notes.

10. Write notes in words or phrases. Do not use complete sentences. Write them in the quickest way that makes sense.

TECHNOLOGY ADAPTATION

- Work with a partner to create a Google Doc. Summarize the information from this unit within the electronic document. Display creativity by using words as well as electronic nonlinguistic representations.

UNIT IV
ORGANIZING THE PARAGRAPH

There are four criteria to use when organizing a paragraph—topic sentence, support, unity, and coherence. When you learn to use these when writing, you will develop both composition and thinking skills related to the organization and clear presentation of a position or argument.

The Paragraph Detective (Part I)

Directions: Each of the two paragraphs below has one major error or weakness in the way it is written. Read each paragraph carefully, and briefly describe what you think is wrong with it. Write your descriptions on the lines below the paragraphs.

Paragraph A

(1) It developed from a mixture of country-western music, played by whites, and African American rhythm and blues. (2) Teenagers first heard the records on the radio, liked the lively beat of the music, and started to buy them. (3) One of the biggest attractions of the new music was the way people could dance to it. (4) The performers were mostly young men in their late teens and early twenties, people like Chuck Berry, Little Richard, Bill Haley, and Buddy Holly. (5) The singer who became the most famous and successful was Elvis Presley, who was a genuine sensation for many years. (6) By the end of the 1950s, he had sold $120 million worth of records.

_____

_____

_____

Paragraph B

(1) Many people don't like cold winters, but I think they're great because of all the winter sports I enjoy. (2) Where we live, winter starts in November and lasts at least until March. (3) Often the temperature stays below the freez-

ing point for weeks on end. (4) When that happens all the ponds and streams freeze over with a thick layer of ice. (5) Also, when snow falls, it usually stays around until spring comes to melt it away.

_____

_____

_____

WHAT IS A PARAGRAPH?

The first basic building block of good writing is the *complete sentence*. The second one is the *paragraph*. A paragraph is a group of sentences that are organized around *one* main idea and that work together to explain, describe, or discuss that idea.

REMEMBER: A good paragraph has one main idea. Once you have learned to write good paragraphs, you have the key skill to do any kind of writing that you will ever want to do.

WHAT ARE THE ELEMENTS OF A GOOD PARAGRAPH?

Topic Sentence

A *topic sentence* is a sentence that clearly tells the reader what the paragraph is about. It expresses the main idea or topic of the paragraph. Usually it is the first sentence in the paragraph.

Exercise I

Directions: On the lines below, write a good topic sentence for paragraph A of "The Paragraph Detective (Part I)."

_____

_____

_____

Support

The topic sentence gives the main idea of the paragraph. All the other sentences in the paragraph should give details and examples that describe, back up, or explain the main idea. This giving of details and examples is called *support*. In the following "Example Paragraph," see how all the sentences tell you more about the topic sentence.

Example Paragraph

Working as a golf caddy is the best job I've ever had. I've met a lot of interesting people and have also learned a great deal about the game of golf. Once I actually had the chance to caddy for a pro who has won five major tournaments. Caddying is always outdoor work, which I really appreciate, particularly on beautiful summer days. The job provides me with a lot of exercise, too. Walking the golf course several times a day can easily add up to 20 miles or more. Finally, the pay is good, and there are some excellent fringe benefits, like tips and gifts of old golf equipment.

Exercise II

Directions: Write two sentences that give support to the topic sentence in paragraph B.

1. _____
_____
_____

2. _____
_____
_____

The Paragraph Detective (Part II)

Directions: Each of the two paragraphs below has one major error or weakness in the way it is written. Read each paragraph carefully, and briefly describe what you think is wrong with it. Write your descriptions on the lines below the paragraphs.

Paragraph C

(1) I first learned to like camping in the mountains during the summer I worked in Wyoming. (2) Every Friday afternoon while I was there, Mrs. Crenshaw would drive me and at least one of the other girls up to the end of High Valley Road. (3) You might have seen that road on TV because they have filmed a couple of TV movies in that area. (4) Then we'd hike in following the Little Muddy Creek Trail until we reached the shores of Beaver Lake. (5) It was a tough climb at first, particularly with a full pack on my back. (6) My pack is a Gerry Mountaineer, green with red stripes. (7) But as the summer went on, I got used to the weight and became a better climber as well. (8) After about three hours of climbing, we'd reach the lake and make camp. (9) Then we would have that night, all day Saturday, and Sunday morning before we had to climb back down to the road. (10) The time I spent up there in the mountains swimming, hiking around, cooking my own food, and just being alone in the wilderness was the best part of my summer. (11) I like hot dogs and beans a lot.

_____
_____
_____

Paragraph D

(1) There are many ways to bake bread, but the method I use is called the No Failure Method because you can't go wrong if you follow the directions. (2) First you mix the yeast, honey, milk, water, and half the flour. (3) Beat this mixture together well, and then let it rise in a warm place for one hour. (4) Then you add the oil and the other half of the flour. (5) Roll the dough into a ball, and knead it for at least 10 minutes. (6) Let it rise twice, each time for another hour. (7) Then fashion the dough into loaves, and bake them at 350 degrees for 45 minutes. (8) When you knead the dough, make sure you work it all together thoroughly. (9) Don't put in too much oil, or the bread will taste greasy. (10) Be sure to use water and milk that's warm but not hot to the touch.

_____

_____

_____

_____

Unity

The word *unity* means oneness, that different things are all part of the same larger whole. Unity in a paragraph means that all the ideas and information in that paragraph are directly related to the main idea expressed in the topic sentence. (The "Example Paragraph" has unity. It is a *unified* paragraph.)

Exercise III

Directions: On the line below, write the numbers of the sentences in paragraph C of "The Paragraph Detective (Part II)" that are not in *unity* with the rest of the paragraph.

_____

Coherence

The word *coherence* means sticking together. In a paragraph, coherence means that each sentence should "stick" to the sentence that comes before it; that is, each sentence should follow the previous one in a way that makes sense. (The "Example Paragraph" has coherence. It is a *coherent* paragraph.)

Exercise IV

Directions: On the line below, write the numbers of the sentences in paragraph D that are not coherent with the rest of the paragraph.

_____

A WAY TO ORGANIZE PARAGRAPHS

Writing good paragraphs begins with organizing your ideas. This is a skill that you can learn. The method of organizing your ideas described below can help you to express your ideas and feelings in writing more clearly and effectively.

Here are the steps for organizing a paragraph:

1. First, think about what you want to say. Ask yourself: What are the ideas and/or feelings that I want to communicate?

2. Ask yourself: What is the main idea of this paragraph? Think about what the possibilities are. Then decide what the main idea is, and jot it down on a piece of paper.

3. Write down a few words about each detail and example that you want to include in the paragraph. This will give you an outline from which to write.

   Example Outline:

   A. Main idea: Why take vacations in Canada

      1. Detail: Mountains—climbing, skiing

      2. Detail: Lakes—swimming, boating

      3. Detail: Big cities—Toronto, Montreal, Vancouver

      4. Detail: French Canadian culture—Quebec

4. Take your main idea and write it as a *topic sentence.*

   Example of a topic sentence: There are many good reasons for taking your vacation in Canada.

5. Then write the rest of your paragraph, working from the outline that you made before. Be sure to include all the details and examples from your outline in your paragraph.

Read over what you've written and check for *support, unity,* and *coherence.* If your paragraph doesn't say what you want it to say, rewrite it.

Exercise V

Directions: Write an outline for a paragraph describing what you think you will be like when you are 21 years old. Include at least three details that support your main idea.

Main idea _____

_____

Supporting detail 1. _____

_____

Supporting detail 2. _____

_____

Supporting detail 3. _____

_____

Supporting detail 4. _____

_____

Supporting detail 5. _____

_____

Supporting detail 6. _____

_____

Exercise VI

Directions: Reread the "Example Paragraph" following Exercise I. On the lines below, write a summary of the paragraph. Be sure to capture the main idea(s) and use synonyms where possible. You might consider using a thesaurus or dictionary while completing this exercise.

_____

_____

_____

_____

SUMMARY

The two basic building blocks of good writing are as follows:

- Complete sentences

- The paragraph

A paragraph is a group of sentences that are organized around one main idea. Here are the elements of a good paragraph:

1. Topic sentence: A sentence that clearly states what the paragraph is about, usually placed at the beginning of the paragraph.

2. Support: Details and examples that describe, back up, or explain the topic sentence.

3. Unity: All the sentences are directly related to the main idea expressed in the topic sentence.

4. Coherence: Each sentence follows the one before it in a way that makes sense.

Writing good paragraphs begins with organizing your ideas. You can use the method described below to organize your ideas before you write, and then write a paragraph.

1. First, think about what you want to say.

2. Write down the main idea of the paragraph. Then jot down the details and examples that you want to include under it. This will give you a working outline.

3. Take your main idea and write it as a topic sentence. Then, using your outline as a guide, write the rest of the paragraph.

4. Read over what you have written and check for support, unity, and coherence.

TECHNOLOGY ADAPTATION

- Write a short story on the topic of your choice. Share it with a class partner in an online blog site. Have the other student peer review and comment back to you using electronic revision comments and suggestions.

- Create a "topic web" using a commercial software application such as Microsoft Word. You can also download graphic organizers from the Internet to create a web. The web should feature a central topic, supporting details, and other pertinent information related to your topic. Make the topic web eye catching, colorful, and easy to follow. Make sure you have enough details on your "branches."

UNIT V
VOCABULARY: GETTING MEANING FROM CONTEXT

INTRODUCTION

"Getting meaning from context" is the vocabulary learning and study skill of examining context to develop a working definition for an unknown or unfamiliar word. The use of this skill is associated both with students who are academically successful and with people who value and enjoy reading. The difference in your vocabulary level is directly related to academic achievement.

Efficiently learning vocabulary terms and words will help to increase the effectiveness of your ability to read. When you encounter an unknown word, you may choose either to ignore it or to disrupt the flow of your reading by looking it up at that moment in a dictionary or thesaurus. When you use context clues to develop some understanding of the word, the process of reading can continue without interruption and will offer greater involvement, meaning, and reward. You can look up the word at an appropriate later time if desired.

GETTING STARTED

Your vocabulary is your language. It is all the words you understand and can use in speaking, writing, reading, and listening. If you only "sort of know" a word's meaning but cannot use that word yourself, then it is not really a part of your vocabulary. Usually people need to see and use a word several times before they really know what it means.

This unit will show you a learning skill that can help you increase your vocabulary and make your reading more interesting and enjoyable.

EXTRACTING MEANING FROM CONTEXT CLUES

When reading, you will come across words that are unfamiliar or unknown. There are two good ways to learn about the meaning of an unknown word:

1. *Look it up in the dictionary.* Looking it up immediately is particularly useful when needing to know an exact definition or pronunciation of the word.

2. *Try to figure out its meaning from context clues.* CONTEXT means the setting in which something is found. For example, a person lives in the context of his or her family. A clue in a mystery is only meaningful in the

35

context of other information. In language, context means the words and sentences around any particular word. CONTEXT CLUES are familiar words and phrases in a sentence or paragraph. These are words the reader knows. From these familiar words, the reader can often figure out the meaning of an unknown word.

Read the paragraph below carefully. On the line beneath it, write the meaning of the word *incessant*. Use context clues to help discover that meaning.

EXAMPLE: She had a CD player that held nine disks and played them one after another. When the last one finished, the first CD started again. So the music coming from her room was *incessant*.

incessant means _____

KINDS OF CONTEXT CLUES

There are four kinds of context clues in this unit:

- Definition or restatement

- Example or description

- Comparison or contrast

- Inference

Definition or Restatement

Sometimes a sentence or paragraph actually includes a definition of the unknown word. It is usually not a dictionary definition, but it does tell you the meaning of the word.

Example of a Definition as a Context Clue

If your house *depreciates*, that means that it loses some of its value.

depreciate means _____

At times authors will use a difficult or uncommon word and feel a need to explain its meaning. One way in which they do this is *restatement*: to include the meaning of the difficult word in the same sentence in which they use that word. Another way in which they do this is to include a synonym for the difficult word in the same sentence.

Example of a Restatement as a Context Clue

One of the weapons available to a government is *propaganda*, the spreading of its own narrow and often false views.

propaganda means _____

Exercise I

Directions: Circle the words in each sentence that are context clues to the meaning of the italicized word.

1. A *facsimile* is always an exact copy.

2. They had already begun to *dismantle* the ship, taking it apart piece by piece.

3. The workers built a *trestle*, a braced framework made of wood, as a support for the railroad tracks where they crossed a stream.

4. A *hypothesis* is a proposed explanation for an event or a group of events. It is often used to guide investigation in scientific study.

Example or Description

In its context, an unknown word may be followed by examples that can give you an idea of what the word means. The examples may also come before the unknown word. With this kind of context clue, you can gain a sense of what the unfamiliar word means by looking at the examples.

Example of Examples as Context Clues

The *sweatshops* where many poor immigrants worked were characterized by overcrowding, poor heat and ventilation, no fire escapes, and very low wages.

sweatshop means _____

Another kind of context clue–like examples is a description, a clause or phrase that tells the meaning of an unknown word. A description gives a word picture of something or shows some of its parts. The description usually comes after the unknown word.

Example of a Description as a Context Clue

When I *procrastinate* and put off working on a project day after day until just before it is due, I usually don't do as good a job as I am capable of doing.

procrastinate means _____

Exercise II

Directions: Write a definition for each italicized word below on the lines provided. Use context clues to develop a definition. Circle the words in the sentences that gave you clues as to the meaning.

1. Should our society have a *censor* who would decide what books and movies should not be available to children?

   censor means _____

2. Animals are divided into invertebrates and *vertebrates*. Monkeys belong to the *vertebrates* because they have backbones.

   vertebrates means _____

3. Squares, rectangles, and trapezoids are all *quadrilaterals*.

   quadrilateral means _____

4. Some dishonest winemakers have been known to *adulterate* their expensive wines by adding water or cheaper wine to them.

   adulterate means _____

Comparison or Contrast

One kind of context clue is given when the author tells you about an unknown word by *comparing* it with something else. A comparison tells the reader what something is like. By knowing what something is similar to, the reader can often gain a sense of what it is.

Example of a Comparison as a Context Clue

Her *predicament* presented her with the same difficult problem she had faced the year before when her family had moved for the first time.

   predicament means _____

Another kind of context clue is given when the author tells you about an unknown word by *contrasting* it with something else. A contrast tells the reader what something is not like. By knowing what something is different from, the reader can often get an idea of what it is.

Example of a Contrast as a Context Clue

Instead of being *demoted* as she had feared, she was offered a new and more challenging job that paid more.

demoted means _____

Exercise III

Directions: Read the following sentences and circle the words from the context of the sentence that provides hints for the definition. Using the lines provided, write a definition for each italicized word below. Use context clues to develop definitions.

1. Rather than the usual 20 devoted fans, the basketball team found a large *throng* awaiting their return at the airport.

   throng means _____

2. Her *prowess* on the parallel bars is like the skillful daring of a great acrobat.

   prowess means _____

3. This year's yard sale was a *fiasco*. They earned even less money than they did last year.

   fiasco means _____

4. At first people thought that television would make radio *obsolete*, but it's turned out that millions of people still listen to radio.

   obsolete means _____

Inference

An *inference* is a conclusion or idea the reader creates by examining various facts and then making a reasonable judgment based on those facts. For example, the reader can often *infer* what the menu will be at lunch by walking past the cafeteria and recognizing the smells of the various foods.

Sometimes you can infer the meaning of an unknown word by examining the meanings of the words and phrases around it.

Example of an Inference as a Context Clue

If you have ever gone on a blind date, you've probably experienced that moment of *trepidation* just before you meet your date for the first time.

trepidation means _____

Exercise IV

Directions: Read the following sentences and pay particular attention to the words in italics. Write a definition for each italicized word below on the lines provided. When developing the definitions, circle the words within each sentence that provided clues to the meaning.

1. I'm a very friendly person. I always like to be with people, either doing things that we enjoy or just talking. I suppose that's why people say I'm *gregarious*.

   gregarious means _____

2. There are still no cures for the common cold. The medicines that people take for a cold are simply *palliatives* that help them to feel a little better for a few hours at a time.

   palliative means _____

3. The *tortuous* road we had to climb had one steep and narrow curve after another all the way to the top. That's probably why it's called Snake Hill Road.

   tortuous means _____

4. I like Mary because she's not *exclusive*. When she has a party, she invites the whole class, not just her best friends.

   exclusive means _____

HINTS FOR USING CONTEXT CLUES

1. When encountering an unknown word, looking it up in the dictionary may interfere with the flow of reading. Try to use context clues to get a sense of the unknown word's meaning while continuing to read.

2. You may figure out the meaning of an unknown word from context clues and can quickly jot that word down. Then, when a natural break in reading occurs, look the word up in the dictionary or a thesaurus. Check to see how close the context definition is to the dictionary definition.

3. When still unsure of the meaning of an unknown word from context clues, look up the word and learn what it means.

Exercise V

Directions: Write a definition for each italicized word below on the lines provided. Use context clues to develop definitions. Circle or highlight the words in each sentence that provided hints as to the meaning.

1. They were lying on their stomachs, *inert*, like dead men except for the soft hum of their breathing.

   inert means _____

2. They had to bring in *mercenaries* or hired soldiers to fight the war.

   mercenary means _____

3. The *surveillance* of the suspect's house went on for more than a week, but the police learned nothing new from all their hours of waiting and watching.

   surveillance means_____

4. After working for two years in the dark, overheated office, Felicia developed such a *loathing* for the place that she vowed to find another job as soon as she possibly could.

   loathing means _____

5. The talk show host always *gesticulated* as she spoke, moving her arms and hands to help her welcome guests, praise them, ask them questions, and even make fun of them.

   gesticulate means _____

6. Our lungs and other parts of the *respiratory* system enable us to breathe.

   respiratory means _____

7. The mayor's waiting room used to be full of *petitioners* who were seeking special favors.

   petitioner means _____

8. Rather than *disparage* people when they make mistakes, try to praise them when they do things correctly.

   disparage means _____

9. Claude has become such a good mechanic that I can't *differentiate* between his work and work done by the man who owns the garage.

   differentiate means _____

10. The sisters were very different. One was *parsimonious* while the other spent her money like water.

    parsimonious means _____

11. Many animals, such as dinosaurs, are now *extinct.*

    extinct means _____

12. The disease brought with it a feeling of *lassitude*, which made her feel like lying in bed all day.

    lassitude means _____

13. To *emote* or express one's feelings is usually very healthy.

    emote means _____

14. At election time people face a difficult *dilemma* if they don't like any of the candidates who are on the ballot.

    dilemma means _____

15. Jack told his friends that he had already ignored several *provocations*, such as curses directed at him and a snowball thrown at his head.

    provocation means_____

Exercise VI

Directions: Write a definition for each italicized word below on the lines provided. Use context clues to develop definitions. Circle or highlight the words within the sentence that provided clues to the meaning of the italicized word.

1. The president has a group of people who travel with him wherever he goes. Some of them are bodyguards. Others are aides and advisors. Even when he's with his family, this *entourage* is never far away.

   entourage means _____

2. Even as a child Denise liked to watch birds in flight and paint pictures of them. "When I grow up," she told herself, "I'll spend all my time learning about birds." Now, after all these years of preparation, she is finally an *ornithologist*.

   ornithologist means _____

3. Wood is *opaque*. So are concrete and iron. But glass and water are not *opaque*.

   opaque means _____

4. It takes a lot of *stamina* for a runner to complete a marathon. She or he must have both strength and endurance.

   stamina means _____

5. He had known her for little more than a week. He'd only talked with her twice, but he'd already sent her flowers three times. Clearly, he was *infatuated* with her.

   infatuated means _____

6. The lifeguard worked on the man for almost five minutes before she was able to *resuscitate* him.

   resuscitate means _____

7. She explained that she had only two *siblings*, a brother and a sister.

    sibling means _____

8. In April, Roberto spent a week hiking through the mountains alone. Many of his friends thought he was foolish for undertaking such a project. Yet when he returned, they were all eager to know how his *solitary* week had gone.

    solitary means _____

9. Before people learned that the earth was round, they did not know that they could *circumnavigate* the globe in ships.

    circumnavigate means _____

10. Sheila and her friends had gone to the museum without bothering to check the price of admission. They had expected to pay five dollars or more to get in and were happy to learn that there was only a *nominal* charge for students.

    nominal means _____

11. He suffered from *amnesia* and could not remember his name or his address.

    amnesia means _____

12. This document contains every word said in the courtroom. If you read this *verbatim* account of the trial, you will know what went on.

    verbatim means _____

13. The officer thought that Robert was *inebriated* because his car was weaving across the road. It took Robert a long time to convince the officer that he had not been drinking and that the car was weaving because his steering had failed.

    inebriated means _____

14. The students at this school are a *heterogeneous* group. They include people of every race and major religious group in the world.

    heterogeneous means _____

15. She put on her protective gear and headed out to the *apiary* to collect a fresh supply of honey.

    apiary means _____

SUMMARY

One good way to figure out the meaning of an unknown word is to use *context clues.*

The *context* is the setting in which the unknown word is found. It includes the words, phrases, and sentences around the unknown word. Context clues are familiar words and phrases. From the meaning of these, the reader can often figure out the meaning of the unknown word.

The kinds of *context clues* are the following:

1. *Definition or restatement.* The context actually includes a definition of the unknown word. Or, the context gives the reader a restatement of it, expressing its meaning in other words.

2. *Example or description.* The context includes examples of the unknown word that can give the reader an idea of its meaning. Or, the context describes the meaning of the unknown word.

3. *Comparison or contrast.* The context tells the reader what the unknown word is like or what it is not like.

4. *Inference.* The context gives the reader enough information about the unknown word to allow some reasonable conclusions to be drawn.

When reading, try to use *context clues* to gain a sense of the meaning of an unknown or unfamiliar word. Then look up the unknown word in the dictionary. See how close the context definition is to the dictionary definition.

TECHNOLOGY ADAPTATION

- Complete an online crossword puzzle. Start with an easier level, and then progress until the level of difficulty requires the use of a dictionary or other source to help find meanings of phrases or words. The dictionary reference source may also be retrieved from an online source.

- Look at the etymology of words using an online source. Etymology is the history and origin of a word. Using a PowerPoint or other presentation software, the etymology of words can be presented to others.

- Use an online dictionary or reference source and have the software "read" out loud unfamiliar words so they can be heard and properly pronounced.

- Download a public domain source (free download) to a Kindle, Nook, or other commercial reader. Then, use the highlighting feature to help define words in context.

UNIT VI
A WAY TO READ TEXTBOOKS

INTRODUCTION

A large part of the schoolwork that any secondary school student does is reading. You read short stories, novels, newspaper and magazine articles, online articles, poems, plays, and so on, but much of the reading you do is in textbooks.

Exercise I

Directions: Think about the ways that textbooks are different from novels and stories. List three of these differences on the lines below.

1. _____

2. _____

3. _____

4. _____

HOW DO YOU READ A TEXTBOOK?

Many students read a textbook exactly the same way they read a short story or a novel. They start with the first word on the first page and read straight through until they come to the last word of the assignment.

However, as you have seen above, a textbook is very different from a short story or a novel. People write textbooks to help the reader learn the information inside them as easily as possible. Most textbooks are divided into chapters. The chapters, in turn, are divided into sections, which usually have headings above them.

Think of the chapter titles and section headings as *road signs*. They tell you where the textbook is going, what the next chapter or section is about. It makes sense, then, to read a textbook in a special way, one that takes advantage of these signs.

A WAY TO READ TEXTBOOKS

The way of reading textbooks that this unit will show you has three steps:

1. Survey

2. Read and take notes

3. Review

1. Survey

Before you start to read the textbook, take 2–3 minutes to survey your assignment. This means to read the chapter title, introduction, and section headings. Also, be sure to read the summary or conclusion and any review questions at the end of the chapter.

As you survey, ask yourself: What is this reading about? What are the main ideas here? What do I already know about this? What do I need to learn? Ask yourself questions like these, and then answer them.

2. Read and Take Notes

Once you have surveyed a section or chapter in your textbook, the next step is to read it carefully. Also, decide if you want to take notes for this reading. As you have already discovered, taking notes both helps you learn as you read and gives you a record of the reading that you can use later on. When you will need to know about this reading later on, then you will probably want to take notes.

If you are going to take notes, decide which note-taking method you will use. Always read a whole section before you start to take your notes.

3. Review

When you have finished reading your assignment, then it is time to review. *Review* means to take a few minutes and go over the main ideas and important details that you have just read. You can do this in your head, by talking with a friend, and/or by going over your notes.

When you review, ask yourself: What's important for me to learn from this reading? What are the main ideas? Is there anything here that I do not understand? If so, how will I find out about it? Ask yourself questions like these, and then answer them. When you take notes from your readings, you can use your notes as part of your review. Read through your notes to go over the main ideas and make sure that these make sense to you.

Many textbooks include "questions for study" at the end of each chapter. You can also use these questions to help you review. Ask yourself each "question for study," and then answer it. If you cannot answer any of the questions, go back to the reading to find the answer.

Another way to review is to turn each section heading in your reading into a question. Ask these questions based on the section headings, and answer them. If you do not know an answer, review the section until you find it.

The purpose of reviewing is to help you really learn the main ideas and important details that you have just read. When you take a few minutes to review, you will be able to remember much more about what you have read.

Exercise II

Directions: Read the Textbook Section using the three-step method described previously in this unit. If you are uncertain about any of the steps, look back at the explanations. Take notes for this reading in the space provided. Use one of the note-taking methods learned in Unit III.

Textbook Section I

A NEW WAY TO TRAVEL. Automobiles are so important today that it is hard to think of a time when we did not have them. Yet you can find people today who can remember when a car was something new.

The internal combustion engine burns a fuel inside itself and uses the heat to provide power. It was developed in Europe. It opened the way for men to invent the automobile and later the airplane. One of the German-made "horseless carriages" was brought to our country. It was studied by Charles E. and J. Frank Duryea. In 1893, they drove down the streets of their city in a gasoline-powered car they had designed and built.

The next year, in 1894, the Apperson brothers and Jonathan Maxwell built a car planned by Elwood G. Haynes. These men helped start our auto industry. Within a few years, other men, inventors and mechanics, were turning out automobiles of their own. This new business used the skills we had developed in the carriage business. Men like the Studebakers of South Bend, Indiana, found it easy to shift from one business to the other.

Some of our first automobiles were powered by steam or electricity. Cars that used gasoline were much better; before long, we gave up the other types. What did these early cars look like? They were not at all like the ones you see today. They weren't big, shiny, or powerful. Their tires were poorly made. These cars broke down easily on hard drives. You had to be a mechanic to keep one running well. But when they ran, they got you there. People bought them. This was a way to travel!

CHANGES BROUGHT BY THE AUTOMOBILE. In less than twenty-five years, we had given up the use of horses for travel and moving goods. Today, much of our country's wealth depends upon the automobile. It is one of our largest industries. Many other businesses supply the automobile makers. Automobiles need rubber; they need electric equipment; they need cloth, glass, and plastic; they need paint and special metals. As we began to use more automobiles, our country built better-surfaced roads; today we have the best roads in the world.

The automobile has brought us many problems, too. Every year thousands of people are killed or hurt in accidents. More of our people have been killed in cars than in all the wars our country has fought. How can we end this waste of life? We still seek an answer to this great national problem.

Notes for Exercise II

_____

_____

_____

_____

_____

_____

_____

_____

_____

_____

_____

WHAT ARE THE ADVANTAGES OF THE _SURVEY, READ AND TAKE NOTES, REVIEW METHOD?_

1. Using this method can help you become an active reader, one who reads to understand and learn rather than just turning the pages and getting it over with. If you are an active reader, you will find that your reading will be more interesting to you.

2. Using the survey, read and take notes, review method will help you to learn more when you read and remember more about what you have read. This method is designed to make the most of the way your memory works.

3. When you decide to take notes from your reading as a part of this method, you will remember more about what you have read. Also, you will have a record of the reading with which you can study.

4. Although it will probably take you a little more time to use the survey, read and take notes, review method at first, once you learn how to do it, you will find that it can be as fast as your old method . . . and much more effective! Practice this method three or four times, and you will soon see how quickly you can become comfortable with it.

TIPS FOR TAKING NOTES FROM YOUR READING

1. Always use your own words in your notes. Putting ideas and information into your own words is a good way to learn about them.

2. Write your notes in words and phrases, not in complete sentences. Use abbreviations and symbols to save time.

3. Remember that your notes are for you, not for anyone else. Take notes that make sense to you.

Exercise III

Directions: Use the survey, read and take notes, review method to read the textbook sections below. Write your notes for these sections in the space provided.

Textbook Section II

A FLYING MACHINE. People long dreamed of being able to fly. However, they had never had a way to keep a heavier-than-air "ship" up in the air. Then, in 1903, two young bicycle mechanics, Wilbur and Orville Wright, placed a motor on their flying machine. It turned a propeller, which made the air flow in a way that kept their machine up in the air. Their first flight was at Kitty Hawk, North Carolina. They kept their plane in the air for several hundred feet. They had invented the first true airplane.

They were not the first to try. Back in the 1700s balloons had been invented, which were large enough to carry a basket with people in it. Many hoped this would be the beginning of flying. But these balloons were dangerous; it was hard to control their flight.

The next step came after 1800. Men in both Europe and America worked with gliders. These were built of light wood, and used wind currents to keep them up in the air. The Wright brothers had worked with gliders, too. They learned much about what was needed to make an airplane fly. They had to control the wind currents to keep their plane up. They built a boxlike plane and a gasoline engine to power it. Then, even though the world took little notice at first, they made their machine fly.

AVIATION IMPROVES. Aviation is the science of building and flying airplanes. We have learned much about aviation since the days of the Wright brothers. They and other men in many parts of the world worked for the next ten years to make better planes. Then, in 1914, a world war began. Both sides built planes and trained young pilots. The airplanes they flew in that war were slow, and did not fly well. Stories are told of pilots in World War I who flew wingtip to wingtip and fought it out with blazing revolvers!

Aviation boomed after the war. Men set up companies to build and sell airplanes. Daring pilots made long trips. Some died; others became famous. In 1927, young Charles A. Lindbergh surprised the world by flying his plane, the *Spirit of St. Louis*, from New York to Paris, France. He flew alone for 3,610 miles across the Atlantic. His success showed our people that air travel had a great future. More people were willing to invest their money in the new industry.

Notes for Exercise III

_____

_____

_____

_____

_____

_____

_____

SUMMARY

Textbooks are very different from novels, short stories, and plays. Textbooks are written in a special way to help the reader learn the information within them as easily as possible. They are usually organized into chapters and sections, with chapter titles and section headings.

A way of reading textbooks that takes advantage of this organization is the survey, read and take notes, review method.

1. *Survey.* Quickly look over the chapter title, introduction, section headings, and conclusion or summary to get an idea of what the chapter is about. Also, read any questions for study that you find at the end of the chapter.

2. *Read and take notes.* Read the chapter carefully. Take notes if you will need to recall the information in the chapter later on.

3. *Review.* Go over the main ideas and important details in the chapter. Ask yourself: What do I need to learn from this reading? Then answer your question.

TECHNOLOGY ADAPTATION

- Take notes from your textbook using a smart phone, tablet, or computer. Digital notes allow you to organize into multiple files and folders without having to carry so many papers with you.

- Taking notes on a digital device allows you to copy and paste similar sections more easily, color code, and boldface more important information. Typing notes is often faster (if you are a fast typist) than handwriting and the notes are easier to read at a later time.

- Have a digital device ready. Oftentimes, textbooks have more resources and enrichment activities available than just the printed version. You can utilize the Internet and follow the directions of the textbook to access these resources.

UNIT VII
RESEARCHING, READING, AND USING ONLINE TEXTS

INTRODUCTION

In our fast-paced world, the Internet delivers quick and easy access to information. The art of actually reading digital text may seem appealing and what many more of us do now, but the value of using a book for seeking information and learning still has a valid place for students. Reading and using online texts from traditional print mediums versus online formats presents many different challenges for learners. Although the technology and the Internet has made many electronic books, research databases, journals, blogs, and other sources widely available through electronic retrieval, deciphering what is useful and even reliable information is difficult. Further, actually reading online poses its own set of challenges.

Readers who read from a printed book will do so at a slower pace and exhibit greater fatigue in a shorter time frame than when reading online. Most basic-level researchers perform a simple-surface level search of the Internet, read the information retrieved (for pleasure or for research), and then consider that information "good enough" and move on. While this may be suitable, it often does not provide the depth and breadth required for quality learning.

Exercise I

1. Perform a search for the Industrial Revolution. Suggested search engines are Google.com, Bing.com, Yahoo.com, and Ask.com. Search engines usually return ten or so websites per page. Using these results, review three to five of the returned choices. Look for one source that looks like an encyclopedia article on the topic.

2. Determine if the entry is user edited, or if it is from a valid source such as a commercial company like World Book.

3. Next, review a choice that is in the form of a blog or forum where users have commented on the published content.

4. Next, look for a visual source such as YouTube.

5. Finally, look for a web page that displays an entry that was published by a university or other "expert voice."

6. Compare what you have found by creating a T-chart. Do this by drawing a large T on a blank piece of paper, writing "Industrial Revolution" on the top part of the T, and listing similarities on the left column and differences on the right column. Include the URL (this is the http:// address). See the example below.

7. From your notes, determine which site contained the best and most thorough information, which site contained the least detailed, which site was most visually appealing and which was not, and which site had the most content and which had the least.

8. Summarize your findings and come up with a recommendation of which site should be considered a reliable source and explain why.

Exercise II

1. Find a classic book from the library, such as Hawthorne's *The Scarlet Letter*. Read the first few pages of the first chapter.

2. Then, find the book online and read the same passage. Classic books are usually available in the public domain for free.

3. Write a reflection on which text was easier to read and why. What are the pros and cons of reading printed text versus its online equivalent?

4. Summarize your findings.

Exercise III

1. Search for online reading speed and comprehension tests. Suggested search engines are Google.com, Bing .com, Yahoo.com, and Ask.com.

2. Follow the directions of the website to determine your level of reading speed online and the amount you comprehend.

3. Print out your results from the web page (if this option is available).

4. Continue to making reading online a priority so you will improve speed and accuracy.

5. Chart your progress throughout the school year by attempting to read more online offerings.

6. Present your findings at the end of the school year or term.

Exercise IV

1. Using the Internet, do a search of President George Washington. Suggested search engines are Google .com, Bing.com, Yahoo.com, and Ask.com.

2. Retrieve information using at least one electronic journal, one encyclopedia, and one research database.

3. When finished with the search from the Internet, compare results from these three sources retrieved (in small groups).

Exercise V

1. Using the Internet, do a search of President George Washington. Suggested search engines are Google .com, Bing.com, Yahoo.com, and Ask.com.

2. Retrieve information from the first entry the search engine returns.

3. Answer the question, "Is the search engine result from a reliable source for research purposes?" Use the space provided below.

_____

_____

_____

4. In the space provided, write whether the article/source on George Washington is research based or if the source is a contributed site (where anyone can add information to, which may not be reliable or valid information).

_____

_____

_____

Exercise VI

1. Using the Internet, perform a search for at least one website with poor, incorrect, or incomplete information on George Washington. Suggested search engines are Google.com, Bing.com, Yahoo.com, and Ask.com.

2. Compare information from Exercise IV and Exercise V to see how information retrieved from the Internet (if not properly checked from a reliable source) may be invalid.

Exercise VII

1. Choose to read something for pleasure online for at least 30 minutes. Select something age level/grade level appropriate.

2. At the conclusion of the reading session, write a reflection of what you liked and what you disliked about reading for pleasure from a digital medium.

3. Then, read something in traditional print for at least 30 minutes. At the conclusion of the reading session, write a reflection of what you liked and what you disliked about reading for pleasure from traditional print. (It is suggested that you read similar types of material for this exercise.)

4. After completing both reading online and in traditional print format, rank your preference between reading online and reading from print. Indicate your reasons why in the space provided.

_____

_____

_____

SUMMARY

- Reading and using online texts presents many different challenges for students.

- Proper tools and practice can provide a beneficial supplement to sources found in print media.

- The Internet contains a wealth of information—electronic books, research databases, journals, blogs, and other sources widely available free to users.

- Understanding that the Internet is a user-edited phenomenon will help you understand that you must be a discriminating consumer when it comes to text, articles, or facts you find online.

- Practicing using the Internet to read and decipher information will improve your speed and comprehension.

TECHNOLOGY ADAPTATION

- Create an online account with your school or local library. Download content reading to your smart phone, tablet, computer, or other device. Mix your reading with text and online versions. Over a period of time, determine what reading you prefer by your speed, how much you comprehend, and if you are more likely to read using online or printed texts.

- Check with your local newspaper to see if online subscriptions are free or at a reduced rate to students or schools. Make it a goal to read at least three news stories per day. Choose one of a current national event, one of a current local event, and one article of your choosing. If online newspapers are not available, attempt to do this project using a website such as MSN.com, USAToday.com, or news from your local radio or television station.

- On your next school project, use the Internet to conduct research using the school or local library. Explore databases with the help of a librarian or teacher.

MULTIMEDIA PRESENTATIONS

INTRODUCTION

The use of technology makes learning a more visual and interactive process. Everyone can be creative, and the Internet and commercial software allow users the ability to do just about anything when it comes to delivering a multimedia presentation. Software standards like PowerPoint and Internet presentation tools like Prezi and PowToon allow you to make things fun while giving information at the same time. For enhanced video heavy presentations, try Animoto and Movie Maker. Still yet, photos may be manipulated using commercial products like Photoshop while free applications like PicMonkey do similar things in just a few clicks—and without cost to the user.

Multimedia presentations using electronic delivery methods allow users to disseminate information in interesting formats. Further, it allows you to be creative, be engaged, and hook an audience better than more traditional methods. Traditional presentation resources only allowed users to present words and pictures; information is given in silos rather than blended together. Now you have the ability to make a fully interactive presentation, complete with text and information, photos, videos, and graphics. Presentations may be shared with the intended audience, or presentations may be shared via the Internet and distributed to virtually any audience.

SUGGESTED ACTIVITIES FOR UNIT VIII

The following contains a list of suggested directions for Unit VIII. Based on the teacher's directive, be prepared to complete the following activities.

1. Explore different commercial presentation software and presentation applications using the web. Choose from a list of topics related to the given lesson and prepare your own original presentation. The presentation should be simple, information-only presentations to ensure understanding of how to capture their message and use your chosen platform.

2. Using the same presentation previously prepared, incorporate at least three pictures or graphics to enhance your presentation. The pictures/graphics should be modified for effect using one of the example programs listed; or, students may choose to use a different product with teacher approval. The pictures/graphics should enhance the project and provide focus and clarity to the intended audience.

3. Using the same presentation previously prepared, incorporate at least a two-minute motion picture segment. Choose two to four movie clips to support the topic and include at least two minutes of video in your pre-

sentation. If video camera equipment is available, make your own movie for incorporation into the presentation. You may choose to use presentation software available on the school computers, or use free web-based applications. Format the presentation to enhance the product by showing a process, being persuasive like a movie trailer, or being informational.

4. Present your multimedia presentations to the class. Critique and provide input about what worked in the other presentations and what needed improvement.

5. Choose a topic to give a short class presentation, and search the Internet for electronic note-taking applications. If possible, install the program and become familiar with it.

6. Use a system of electronic note-taking for the classroom. Choose one application that is comfortable and provides the most benefit (and is free) and spend a few class sessions learning how to use it. This application may not be applicable in all school situations due to electronic access. If policy allows, use your own device such as a tablet, smart phone, or laptop.

7. Choose your own electronic note-taking software, and prepare a demonstration and training for the class.

8. Learn a combination of note-taking formats: outlining, cloze notes, combination notes, and mapping are some examples.

ADDITIONAL RESOURCES

In order to familiarize yourself with a variety of technological resources, select a resource, research what it can do, and provide a demonstration to the class.

Animoto: an online service that helps create videos from images and video clips.

Blabberize: animate images and make them talk.

Blogspot: allows users to create a simple blog.

Diigo: an online bookmarking service that supports students as they work on a research project.

Edmodo: a resource that provides a way to share classroom content in a way similar to Twitter.

Educreations: tool for sharing video lessons.

Gliffy: collaborative tool for designing flowcharts and diagrams.

Glogster: an online web service that helps create virtual posters through the use of multimedia.

Google Docs: a word processing resource to facilitate sharing, creating, and editing documents.

Google Plus: facilitates the use of video chats.

Lucidchart: create online diagrams and flowcharts.

MyFakeWall: fake Facebook-style profiles for historical figures.

Photovisi: photo collages for downloading and printing.

PicMonkey: photo editing.

Plurk: a social network similar to Twitter.

Posterous: an easy tool for blogging.

ProConLists: an electronic listing of positives and negatives of an issue.

Queeky: an online drawing application.

ReadWriteThink: creates cartoons with images and thought bubbles.

RubiStar: an online tool to help design scoring rubrics.

Schoology: a website designed to manage lessons, engage students, and share content.

Shape Collage: facilitates in making an electronic collage.

StudyBlue: online flash cards, quizzes, and study guides for sharing.

SurveyMonkey: creates a survey and analyzes the results.

TeacherTube: a video-sharing website designed specifically for classroom use.

Tumblr: an easy tool for blogging.

Twitter: an easy-to-use microblog.

Wallwisher: creates a multimedia wall for students to brainstorm ideas, notes, etc.

WebQuest: facilitates students as they research content online.

Wordle: a resource that generates word clouds from text.

Zapd: a tool for creating a website.

SUMMARY

Supporting student learning through a variety of electronic resources is a twenty-first-century skill for both teachers and students. Students must be prepared to learn with multimedia as well as be able to demonstrate learning through the same.

Most professions use electronic resources for sharing information, receiving information, or learning. Journalism, engineering, medicine, education, entertainment, and a variety of other commercial industries all use multimedia to produce, advertise, and sell products and services. The challenge for students and educators is not necessarily learning and knowing how to use these resources; rather, the challenge will be to stay up to date with what is available, most useful, and trending.

TECHNOLOGY ADAPTATION

Not applicable.

PREPARING FOR AND TAKING TESTS: OBJECTIVE QUESTIONS

HOW DO YOU PREPARE FOR A TEST?

Think about how you prepare for a test. What do you do to get ready before you take the test? What kinds of resources do you use to study? And how do you use them? How much time do you give to preparing for a test? Do you study alone or with others?

Imagine that you will have a whole-period test in this class a week from today. On the lines below, briefly describe how you would prepare for it.

_____

_____

_____

_____

_____

PREPARING FOR A TEST

How you prepare for a test has a lot to do with how well you will do on it. Later in this unit, you will read some ideas about how you can better prepare for tests. Then you will be asked to think about these ideas in relation to what you have described above.

WHAT ARE OBJECTIVE QUESTIONS?

Objective questions usually try to find out if you know facts or other kinds of specific information. They may also test more general understandings and skills. Usually, for an objective question, there is only one correct answer for which you will receive credit.

Objective questions often do not require much writing in their answers. You may be asked to write a word or two in a blank or even a few sentences. Frequently, objective questions only ask you to pick a word, a letter, or a number that represents the answer. On a standardized test, you may be asked to fill in a blank square or circle next to the correct answer.

The most commonly used kinds of objective questions are the following:

- Multiple choice

- Matching

- Short answer

- True/False

WHAT CAN YOU LEARN ABOUT OBJECTIVE QUESTIONS THAT WILL BE HELPFUL?

There are methods you can learn to use that will help you in answering each kind of objective question. These methods are not a substitute for preparing for the test by learning the material on which you will be tested. However, they can help you use what you do know more effectively when you are taking a test.

This unit includes a method or methods for answering each kind of objective question.

MULTIPLE CHOICE

Multiple choice questions ask you to choose the right answer from a number of possible answers. This is one of the most frequently used kinds of questions, and it can be tricky, even when you know the right answer. The method described below is one good way to go about answering multiple choice questions.

How to Answer Multiple Choice Questions

1. First, read the question carefully.

2. Try to anticipate the answer in your mind before you start to look at the choices. When you can anticipate the answer and find it among the choices, it's likely to be correct.

3. Read all the choices given, and try to find the right answer. Even if you are sure that the first or second choice is correct, read over all the other choices just to be certain. They may all be correct, and the last choice may be "all of the above."

4. If you don't know which choice is correct after you've read all of them, try this:

   Use a process of elimination. First, cross off all the choices that you know to be wrong. Often this will leave you with only two possible choices left. Pick the one that you think is best.

5. If you have no idea which choice is correct, guess (unless there is a penalty for guessing). Guessing usually does not hurt your score, and you might guess the correct answer.

EXAMPLE: When people are in high school, they are:

(A) 18 years old (B) 16 years old (C) 15 years old (D) 17 years old (E) all of the above

Exercise I

Directions: Answer each of the following questions by circling the correct answer.

A. How many states have capital cities?

(A) 50 (B) 48 (C) half (D) most (E) a lot

B. Anyone born in the United States of America and over 35 years of age can legally be:

(A) an American citizen (B) a doctor (C) male or female (D) president (E) all of the above

C. People first started to watch a lot of television in:

(A) 1899 (B) the 1950s (C) 1776 (D) the 1920s (E) 1964

D. The best method to use in answering multiple choice questions is to:

(A) guess a lot

(B) pick the first answer that seems right

(C) read through all the choices and pick the best one

(D) start with the last question and work backward

(E) none of the above

Narrowing Down the Choices

How do you narrow down the choices when you use a process of elimination? Multiple choice questions often give you information in the question itself that can help you narrow down the choices. You need to figure out the following:

(1) What information is given in the question?

(2) How you can use it?

For example, read the question below.

Anne Hutchinson was driven from the Massachusetts Bay Colony because she taught people:

(A) to live by the Golden Rule

(B) how to buy a good used car

(C) survival skills in desert climates

(D) to stand up for their beliefs, come what may

The question itself tells you the following: Anne Hutchinson was living in the Massachusetts Bay Colony, she lived during colonial times (before 1776), and she was driven from there because of her teachings.

With this information, you can begin to narrow down the choices in terms of:

• Historical probability: Could it have happened at this place, in this time? (This is particularly useful on social studies tests.)

• Common sense: Is the answer reasonable? Or, is it silly or foolish?

Exercise II

Directions: Narrow down the choices in the above question about Anne Hutchinson. Eliminate the choices you believe are historically unlikely. Now, use the same "narrowing down" method for questions 1–4 below. Draw a line through the letter before each choice that you eliminate.

1. George Washington's false teeth were made of:

   (A) soap (B) plastic (C) iron (D) wood (E) aluminum foil

2. If both the president and the vice president of the United States were to die, who would become president?

   (A) the Speaker of the House

   (B) the governor of California

   (C) Abraham Lincoln

   (D) the Queen of England

   (E) the commissioner of the National Football League

3. Most people in the United States commute to work in/on:

   (A) airplanes

   (B) buses and trains

   (C) boats

   (D) cars

   (E) bicycles

4. The primary purpose for a kangaroo's pouch is to:

   (A) protect its young

   (B) store food

   (C) take fewer but longer trips

   (D) all of the above

MATCHING

Matching questions usually give you two lists of information and ask you to connect them with each other in some way.

When you answer a matching question, first read the directions carefully. Then use a process of elimination to answer the question, as follows:

1. Complete the matches that you know first, and cross them off.

2. Then do the best you can with whichever words are left in each column. If you're not sure, guess (unless there is a penalty for guessing).

EXAMPLE: Write the number of each animal in the blank to the left of the word that names a part of that animal.

1. dog   _____ hands

2. opossum   _____ spinnerets

3. horse   _____ wings

4. spider   _____ paws

5. bird   _____ mane

6. human   _____ pouch

Exercise III

Directions: Write the number of each city in the blank to the left of the state in which that city is located.

1. Chicago   _____ Maine

2. New York   _____ Texas

3. Boise   _____ Louisiana

4. Tulsa   _____ Illinois

5. Baton Rouge   _____ California

6. Bangor   _____ Idaho

7. Amarillo   _____ New York

8. Ukiah   _____ Oklahoma

SHORT ANSWER

With short answer questions, you need to know the answer. There are no choices given to you. However, if you don't know the exact answer but do know something related to it, write down what you do know. You may get partial credit for it. Also, guess if you don't know the answer (unless there is a penalty for guessing).

Exercise IV

Directions: Fill in the blank with the right answer.

1. There are _____ whole numbers between one and ten, not including one or ten.

2. How did the first Europeans get to America?

_____

3. People in Great Britain drive on the _____ side of the road.

TRUE/FALSE

- True/false questions are statements that you are asked to judge. Are they true or false?

- True/false questions may seem easy, but they can also be very tricky and difficult. The single most important point to remember in doing these questions is this: for a statement to be true, it must be entirely true.

- Be careful with statements that have one true part and one false part. IF ANY PART OF A STATE-MENT IS FALSE, THEN IT IS A FALSE STATEMENT.

- Be careful with statements that include the words *all*, *always*, *only*, or *never*. They are often false.

EXAMPLE: Write "true" or "false" in the blank following each statement according to your judgment of its truth.

_____ All statements that have the word *never* in them are false.

_____ The sun is bigger than the moon, and the moon is bigger than the earth.

Exercise V

Directions: Each of the 13 statements below deals with suggestions for preparing to take tests or for taking objective tests. Read them carefully. Then mark them "T" for true or "F" for false.

1. It is helpful to know what kind of test your teacher is going to give you. _____

2. Teachers almost never give clues beforehand about what's going to be on a test. _____

3. People learn most efficiently by studying for one long period of time the night before a test. _____

4. The best way to study is to reread your notes and assignments. _____

5. It's very helpful to try to anticipate what questions your teacher will ask you on the test and then tell yourself the answers to those questions when you're studying. _____

6. A good way to prepare for a test is to watch the late show with your friends and eat breakfast in the morning. _____

7. A good way to study is to review your notes, ask yourself questions based on your notes and answer them, and identify what the key concepts and details are in your notes. _____

8. Students who worry a lot about tests always do better. _____

9. You should always study for a test by yourself. _____

10. You should begin to answer the first question on the test right after you read it. _____

11. Read all the directions on the test carefully. Then follow them exactly. _____

12. Guess whenever you don't know the answer unless there's a penalty for guessing. _____

13. Do the hardest questions first. That way you'll get the hardest questions out of the way. _____

Exercise VI

Directions: Think about the suggestions for preparing for a test. Then go back and reread what you wrote about how you get ready for a test. On the lines below, briefly describe at least two new ways of preparing for a test that you will try.

_____

_____

_____

_____

_____

How Can I Prevent Test Anxiety?

_____

_____

_____

_____

_____

TEST DAY

On test day, students can do several things to lower anxiety and prepare mentally.

- Get to class as early as possible. Rushing in late is unsettling and can have a negative impact on performance.

- While waiting on class to begin, recite notes out loud.

- Take deep breaths, close eyes, flex all muscles, and count backward from 100 while inhaling and exhaling deeply.

- Wait for the teacher to review the directions. Do not begin answering any questions without thoroughly reviewing all test directions.

- If mnemonic devices were used to assist with memorization, jot them down in the paper's margins.

- Skim the entire test before beginning.

- Look for point allotment and spend the most time on the ones worth the most points.

- Search for clues within the test for answers.

LEARNING FROM THE TEST

There are a number of things students can do to learn from the test after it is graded and returned.

1. Look carefully to review any comments or suggestions from the instructor.

2. Review individual questions and determine if they were based upon class discussions, lectures, lab experiments, textbooks, or supplemental reading. Then, make a mental note of how to modify (if necessary) study techniques for upcoming examinations.

3. If time was an issue during test completion, consider how time might have been managed more efficiently.

4. Read the test carefully again to determine if any questions were missed due to a misunderstanding or misinterpretation of the directions.

5. Think back to how you felt during the test. Were you tired, hungry, or anxious? If so, those strong emotions can affect the grade on an exam.

6. Consider how many test answers were based upon the understanding of vocabulary words. Vocabulary words are always fair game on a test. When limited with time to study, try to learn as many vocabulary words as possible from the unit of study.

Exercise VII

Directions: Plan of Action—Based upon the information learned from examining a returned test, work with a partner and develop a plan for how you might do better on the next exam. Be specific with your plan of action related to test preparation.

_____

_____

_____

_____

_____

_____

_____

_____

_____

_____

SUMMARY

Objective questions usually have one correct answer for which you will receive credit. There are four main kinds of objective questions. You can learn methods for answering them that will help you on a test.

There are four main kinds of objective questions:

1. *Multiple choice.* Read the question carefully. Try to think of the answer before you look at the choices. Read all the choices given. If you don't know the answer after you've read the choices, use a process of elimination. Cross off the choices you know to be wrong. Pick the most sensible one that remains. When you can, use information in the question itself to help you narrow down the choices.

2. *Matching.* Do the ones you know first, and cross them off. Then do the best you can with whatever ones are left.

3. *Short answer.* If you don't know the exact answer, write down anything you do know that's related. You may get partial credit.

4. *True/False.* Read the statements very carefully. Remember, all parts of a statement must be true for the statement to be true.

There are three basic rules related to preparing for a test:

1. Begin studying from the first day of class.

2. Do not get behind with assignments.

3. Spend a few minutes each day reviewing notes, assignments, and the text.

How you prepare for a test has a lot to do with how well you'll do on it. The more skillfully you prepare, the better you'll do.

TECHNOLOGY ADAPTATION

- Create a PowerPoint or multimedia presentation designed to explain to a classmate how to study for an objective assessment.

UNIT X
PREPARING FOR AND TAKING TESTS: ESSAY QUESTIONS

ANSWERING ESSAY QUESTIONS

The method you learned in Unit IV for organizing a paragraph is also effective when you answer an essay question on a test. As you work through this unit, you will see how you can use this method to help you answer essay questions.

WHAT IS AN ESSAY QUESTION?

An essay question asks you to write a composition of at least one paragraph and often several paragraphs during the test time itself.

An essay question usually asks you to organize what you know and understand about a topic and then express it in a way that responds to that particular question. Most essay questions focus on ideas and understandings, not on facts. Yet you need to include facts in your essay answers when the facts are supporting details that prove your points.

Three examples of essay questions:

- Explain the process of river erosion.

- Compare and contrast the two main characters in *The Outsiders* by S. E. Hinton.

- Discuss the role that computers play in American schools.

A METHOD FOR WRITING ANSWERS TO ESSAY QUESTIONS

Before the Test

- When your teacher schedules a test, find out whether the test will include essay questions. You can answer these questions more efficiently when you prepare for them in advance.

- When you study, try to anticipate the essay questions that your teacher will ask. Ask yourself: What does he or she think is really important in this chapter or unit? How will he or she ask about this?

- Think about how you would answer the essay questions you have posed. Tell yourself the answers you would write. If you need to look anything up to complete these answers, be sure to do that. You will be surprised at how good you can get at figuring out the questions ahead of time.

When You First Get the Test

- When you first get the test, read the directions carefully. If you have a choice of essay questions, read all the questions first. Then choose the ones you can best answer.

- Some tests tell you how much each question is worth. If possible, plan to give a certain amount of time to each question based both on how much that question is worth and how well you think you can answer it.

- Start by working on the question that you can do best (but be careful not to spend too much time on it). This will help to get you thinking about the material on the test and build your confidence.

REMEMBER: Spending a minute or two in planning your time when you have several essays to write is well worth it. Planning your time in this way can help you make sure that you answer all the questions or, at least, those that will benefit you the most.

How to Organize Your Essay

To write an essay on a test, you can use exactly the same method you used to organize and write a paragraph. You will have to work more quickly on a test, but you can follow the same steps, as listed below:

- Read the question carefully. Then think about what you want to say in response to the question.

- Jot down a brief outline of your answer.

- Write your answer.

- If you have time, read over your essay and make any necessary changes or corrections.

The purpose of writing an outline, as noted above, is to help you organize your answer. When you jot down your outline, try to list all the main ideas and important details that you want to include in your answer. At the same time, try to keep your outline brief.

You will find an example of an outline for an answer to an essay question below. The essay question is "Discuss the United States' space program in the 1960s and how it affected life in the United States."

Example of Outline

    I. U.S. space program in the 1960s:

        A. Stimulated by competition with Russians

        B. Unmanned rockets first

        C. Astronauts in orbit around Earth

        D. 1969—landing on moon

   II. How it affected our lives:

        A. Excitement about space

        B. New technology

        C. Satellites—weather forecasting, etc.

        D. Interest in space stations

Exercise I

Directions: Read the essay question below. Think about the question, and decide how you would like to answer it. Then outline your answer on the lines beneath the question.

QUESTION: Describe why the place where you live either is or is not a good place to live.

_____

_____

_____

_____

_____

_____

_____

_____

_____

_____

How to Begin Writing Your Essay

The best way to begin an essay answer is with a *thesis statement*. A *thesis statement* is a sentence that gives the main ideas of your answer. It is like a topic sentence for your answer.

For example, a *thesis statement* for an answer in response about the U.S. space program might be:

The United States' space program in the 1960s moved quickly through several different stages, from tiny, unmanned capsules to a landing on the moon, and had many important effects on people's lives.

Sometimes you can rephrase the essay question itself and use it as part of your thesis statement. For example, the beginning of a thesis statement in an answer to the question in Exercise I might be:

The place where I live is a good place because . . .

How to Use Your Time

Try to divide the time you give to each essay question in the following way. For example, if you have 20 minutes to answer an essay question, you could divide your time as follows:

- Thinking and outlining, 5 minutes

- Writing the essay, 13 minutes

- Reading over and correcting your essay, 2 minutes

REMEMBER: When a teacher grades an essay, more does not mean better. A shorter but well-organized and well-written essay will convey understanding more effectively to the teacher. This kind of essay will almost always earn a higher grade than a longer one that is sloppy and disorganized.

WHAT WORDS ARE USED TO ASK ESSAY QUESTIONS?

Essay questions usually begin with or include a key word that tells you what kind of answer is expected. You need to know what this key word means to answer the question well.

Below you will find a list of words often used to ask essay questions. The teacher will help you understand the meanings of these words.

- Describe—to convey an impression or account of something, usually without judging it; or to tell about what something is, for example, describing a person or a place.

- Summarize _____

- Compare _____

- Contrast _____

- Explain _____

- Evaluate _____

- Criticize _____

- Discuss _____

- Interpret _____

- Justify _____

- Classify _____

- Show _____

- Cause & Effect _____

MORE SUGGESTIONS FOR WRITING ESSAY ANSWERS

1. Before beginning to write, read all the questions. While reading, underline or circle key words that will help to guide your written response.

2. Using scrap paper, the answer sheet, or the test, make a listing of associated words or phrases. Before beginning to write, number the words in a manner that makes sense in terms of answering the question. Then, use the list as an outline for the essay response.

3. For short-answer questions, think before writing and begin by restating the key words of the question, and give succinct and concise answers.

4. Be sure to include both main ideas and supporting details in your answer. The main ideas show that you understand the meaning of the question. The supporting details help to prove the main idea.

5. Stick to your topic as you write. Only answer what the question asks. Do not put in all you know about the subject unless the question calls for that. Writing a brief outline first will help you stick to your topic.

6. If you do not know the entire answer to a question you are working on, start writing what you do know. You may earn partial credit, and the rest of the answer may come to you as you write.

7. Answer in outline form if you lack the time to write out your answer as an essay. The teacher may give you partial credit for showing what you know about the question.

8. Begin with the easiest questions first. This may help to calm any jitters and provide a sense of self-confidence. Additionally, if time is a factor, these questions will be answered, adding to the total points for the exam.

9. Leave space between answers. This will allow information to be added later.

10. Be neat. No one wants to lose points on an essay answer because the teacher could not decipher the student's handwriting.

WHAT CAN YOU DO WHEN A TEST IS RETURNED TO YOU?

There are several ways you can learn from a test your teacher has corrected and returned to you. Can you name two of these ways?

1. _____

_____

_____

_____

_____

2. _____

_____

_____

_____

_____

SUMMARY

An essay question asks you to organize what you know and understand about a topic and to express it in a way that responds to that particular question. Organize the essay answer around the main ideas and include important details that support these main ideas.

Use the same method for organizing and writing the answer to an essay question that you used for writing paragraphs. You will need to work more quickly when you are taking a test, but the method is well worth using.

Below are the steps in the method:

1. Read each essay question carefully. Then think about what you want to say in response to the question.

2. If not noted on the exam, ask for point allotment. Do not make an assumption that all questions are of equal value.

3. Watch for key words that explain exactly what the teacher wants in terms of an answer. If it says, "List," then list. If it says, "Compare and contrast," then compare and contrast; do not merely describe or explain.

4. Write a brief outline of the answer.

5. Budget time. Allow enough time for each question with some time left at the end of class to do a quick review.

6. Begin the essay answer with a thesis statement that states the main ideas of your answer. A thesis statement is like a topic sentence for your answer.

7. Use facts, logic, and evidence. Few, if any, essays ask for a student's "feelings" about a topic.

8. Then write your answer.

9. If time allows, read over the essay and make any necessary changes or corrections.

To answer essay questions well, you need to understand the special words that teachers use to ask these questions. Some of these words are *describe, summarize, compare, contrast, explain, evaluate, criticize,* and *discuss.*

TECHNOLOGY ADAPTATION

- Place students into pairs and ask them to use the Internet to find further information on preparing for essay tests. After information has been located, ask students to record their notes on a class blog.

UNIT XI
LEARNING INDEPENDENCE

INTRODUCTION

It is not uncommon to hear students complain they spend time studying but still do not get the grades they want. This unit is designed to help you focus your attention on studying in a manner that supports learning and higher academic achievement. In other words, by following the suggestions on the next few pages, it will help with basic skills, lifelong learning, and the ability to solve difficult and complex problems.

Students sometimes hear teachers and parents say, "You need to study harder." However, for many students, this is an oversimplification. It is usually not a matter of studying "harder" but rather the recognition of the need to change the type of study method.

This unit is designed to help you help yourself. Most suggestions can be implemented easily and with little effort; however, some will require you to rethink your habits related to studying and learning new information.

SUGGESTED DIRECTIONS FOR UNIT XI

Exercise I

1. Work with a partner and divide the studying tips in the section "Studying Smart" into equal parts. Read half the information with the other partner carefully reading the other half. The purpose for reading the information is to summarize your half and explain it to your partner.

2. After sharing information, circle or highlight the tips most helpful in terms of grades, homework, and academic success.

STUDYING SMART

There are a number of strategies and techniques that help students efficiently and correctly complete assignments. The following Instant Study Skills provide effective suggestions in terms of time and effort.

a. Sit in the front of the classroom. When seated in the front of the classroom there are fewer distractions and temptations in terms of off-task behavior. Though many teachers use seating charts and assign seating based upon a variety of factors, most will accommodate a request to sit in the front, providing they believe it is made for legitimate reasons.

b. Routinely review previous class notes. This can be done before or after class. It can even be done during class when the student believes it is beneficial to do so. Repetition supports learning. Periodically reviewing notes throughout the instructional unit will facilitate retention of content.

c. Copy important points from the whiteboard or PowerPoint. If the instructor believes the information is important enough to display to the class, assume the information might appear again in the form of an assessment instrument.

d. Find a place that is conducive to studying, and consistently use it as such. Individuals are creatures of habit. Good habits related to studying routines and rituals are important. Finding a location used primarily for the purpose of completing homework is a good first step in terms of task accomplishment.

e. Set goals and determine a time for assignment completion. Giving thought to how much time a task will take will help with time management. By virtue of complexity, some projects take longer to complete than others. Break assignments into manageable times, and maintain the self-discipline needed to start and finish in a timely manner.

f. When bored or distracted during study time, briefly set aside the assignment. Stand, walk around the room, or eat something sweet. Just remember to not overuse this strategy at the first sign of fatigue.

g. Self-quiz when reading difficult and complex text. Stop at the bottom of a page and ask what has been learned. Summarize the important points. Take notes or underline.

h. Do not try to read too quickly. It is easy to be discouraged and think the assignment will never be finished. Depending upon the purpose, good readers know rate of reading may need adjustment. If held accountable for the information, read slowly and concentrate carefully on content. Reading in short spurts can help with fatigue and concentration.

i. Do a first review at the end of the reading session. Before putting the text away at the end of a study period, take time to quickly flip through the pages while looking at highlighted material, bold or italicized print, graphics, and captions. This is a good way to provide closure to the activity and support retention.

j. When an assignment is finished ahead of schedule, personal rewards help facilitate a positive attitude. The mental outlook brought to a study session is important to success, so think positively. Few individuals enjoy long hours of concentration and effort related to academic tasks, but most appreciate the feelings that come from accomplishing the assignment in a reasonable amount of time.

k. Avoid underlining or highlighting an entire sentence or paragraph within a text. While underlining and highlighting may be helpful to retention, use it sparingly and do so after finishing the first reading of the material. This will serve as the first review of the content.

l. When taking a test, do the easy questions first. This helps build confidence and can even provide hints to possible answers for more difficult testing items.

m. On an essay exam, do not leave any question unanswered. When an item is left totally blank, a teacher has no choice but to assign a zero. Write something.

n. When taking a test, be careful with handwriting. Nothing is more frustrating for a teacher than struggling to read a student's handwriting. Grading papers and tests is time consuming enough without the added stress of trying to decipher poor penmanship. Do not have an answer marked as wrong because the teacher could not read what was written.

o. On objective tests, do not hesitate to change an answer if warranted. The idea that the first choice is usually the correct one may not necessarily be true. There are a number of reasons why the need to modify an answer might occur. Perhaps something is triggered in the subconscious mind. Maybe there is a hint to an answer from another question within the test. Regardless, changing a previously recorded answer may be well advised.

Exercise II

1. Work with a partner and make a list of what makes it difficult to concentrate.

_____

_____

_____

_____

_____

2. After the list is complete, read and complete "Concentration Is Critical." If you disagree with the statement, be prepared to explain why it is not true for you.

CONCENTRATION IS CRITICAL

For a variety of reasons, some students have difficulty with concentration when attempting to learn something new. Fatigue, stress, irritation, lack of organizational skills, or poor study habits can be problematic.

Read the following statements and decide whether the statement is true for you as a student learner.

Agree or Disagree?

a. Trying to study late into the evening seldom gives much of a return in terms of retention.

____Agree ____Disagree

b. Preview the structure of the text prior to beginning any reading assignment.

____Agree ____Disagree

c.   Immediately rereading a text may not yield the most in terms of learning.

_____Agree _____Disagree

d.   Wait to take notes over a text until the end of a section.

_____Agree _____Disagree

e.   Remember, underlining or highlighting will not support retention as much as written notes.

_____Agree _____Disagree

f.   Do not wait to be in the mood for studying.

_____Agree _____Disagree

g.   Be in the habit of studying at a set time and location.

_____Agree _____Disagree

h.   If content of the text is challenging, find something easier to read on the same subject.

_____Agree _____Disagree

i.   Be aware of noise and the surrounding environment. It is not possible to focus on more than one thing at a time.

_____Agree _____Disagree

j.   Do not study in bed.

_____Agree _____Disagree

k.   When it is necessary to study for an exam and time is in short supply, learn the associated vocabulary words.

_____Agree _____Disagree

l.   Read test directions carefully.

_____Agree _____Disagree

m.   Understand why the information is valuable.

_____Agree _____Disagree

n.   Recognize that reading rate varies, and variation is not necessarily a bad thing.

_____Agree _____Disagree

o.   Use flash cards, vocabulary cards, and term cards.

_____Agree _____Disagree

p.   When studying for a test, try to anticipate possible questions.

_____Agree _____Disagree

q.   Self-quizzing is an important way to review for an exam.

_____Agree _____Disagree

r.   When taking notes on a book or in a class, skip lines between ideas and/or topics.

_____Agree _____Disagree

s.   Resist doodling on notes.

_____Agree _____Disagree

t.   Read the author's questions prior to beginning to read a text.

_____Agree _____Disagree

u.   Avoid procrastination.

_____Agree _____Disagree

v.   Keep a personal calendar.

_____Agree _____Disagree

w.   Begin studying for the exam from the first day of class by frequently reviewing material.

_____Agree _____Disagree

x.   When reading, monitor comprehension.

_____Agree _____Disagree

y. Get plenty of rest and proper nutrition.

_____Agree _____Disagree

Reread the above statements and list the suggestions you would be willing to try immediately.

_____

_____

_____

_____

_____

_____

_____

_____

_____

_____

_____

Exercise III

Directions: Each of the "stories" describes one method a student uses as part of her or his studying routine. Read each "story," and decide whether you think the method used is *good*, *fair*, or *poor*. Write one of these three words in the blank below each "story." Circle or highlight the words or phrases within each example that leads you to believe it is *good*, *fair*, *or poor*.

1. Carmelita sat down at the table after dinner and started to think about what she had to do for school. "Well," she said to herself, "I have to read three pages about decimals in my math book and then do problems 1–10. For history I have to read the first half of chapter 3, the one about the colonies in Virginia and Georgia. Okay, well, the math will take about 45 minutes, and the history will take, oh, maybe half an hour at most. Then I can call up Maria or listen to music." She opened her math book and started to read.

_____

2. Kareem opened his science book to page 34 and started to read with the very first word on the page. He was in a hurry, so he didn't bother even to look at the chapter title or any of the headlines. "Gravity is a force. . . ," he read, and his eyes followed the words down the page. But soon, his thoughts began to wander away from what he was reading. "Will I get that job at the market?" he wondered. "And if I don't, where else can I find a job close to home?" He decided to ask his mother again if he really had to be home for dinner at 6:30 every night. He read for a few more minutes and then began to think about the new girl in his science class. He liked her sense of humor and wondered if she had noticed him. Ten minutes later he finally finished the first section of the chapter and put the book down on his knee. He wanted to rest for a minute before he went on.

_____

3. It was ten minutes to nine, and Sarah had reached the last page of her history reading. "One more page about the New Deal," she thought, "and I'll be done." The reading wasn't so bad, but she really wanted to watch TV at nine. There was a good movie on. Quickly her eyes raced down the last two columns of print. When she reached the end, she yelled, "Made it!" She tossed the book on her bed, raced into the living room, and turned on the television.

SUGGESTIONS FOR HOW TO STUDY

1. How do you begin to study? Before you start to study, ask yourself what you want to accomplish in this study session. Set goals for how long it might take you to do each part of your work. Be sure that your goals are realistic for you. Also, plan to do your hardest work first when you are most alert. Why? If you know what you want to get done and about how long it will take, you can work more efficiently to meet your goals.

2. How do you start an assignment when you want to learn new material? Quickly tell yourself what you already know about the subject of your assignment. Then ask yourself questions like the following ones, and answer them. What do I want to find out about this topic? What am I trying to learn about it? Why do I need to know this information? Knowing what you are trying to learn will help you to focus more clearly on the material that you are studying. It will help you direct your attention to what is important in that material. It will also help you to keep distracting thoughts out of your mind.

3. What do you do when you finish an assignment? When you finish studying something, briefly go over what you have just learned. Talk to yourself about it. Imagine that you are explaining it to someone else. Or, actually find another person to whom you can explain what you have learned. Why? Briefly reviewing what you have just learned will help you to remember it more effectively. A good way to review is to imagine that you are explaining the material to someone else.

Exercise IV

Directions: Read each of the following "stories" and describe one method that a person uses as part of her or his studying. Beneath each "story" you will find a question about the study method described in that "story." Read each "story," and answer each question.

1. Dorice liked to work on algebra problems with her friends, Tina and Vanessa. She found that talking about the problems helped her to understand them better. Besides, it was a lot more fun than sitting by herself. Tonight, however, she had to write a composition for English. Tina and Vanessa wanted to get together while they were writing. Dorice wanted to go, but she knew that she never got any writing done unless she was alone. Finally she decided to go, but her prediction was right. They spent most of the night talking, and Dorice had to write her composition in a hurry when she got home.

   What could Dorice have done to improve her studying that night?

   _____

   _____

   _____

2. On the second day of school, Jack had his first homework assignments for the year. "Oh boy," he thought, "they couldn't even wait until next week to start piling it on. This year," he resolved, "I'm going to start my homework right after dinner and get it done, so I can do what I want to later on. Every night I'll start at the same time," he promised himself.

When he left the table after dinner, Jack rushed to his room and put his books on the table. But before he began, he decided that he just had to call his friend, Todd. One call led to another, and then his brother yelled for him to come and watch a show on TV. At ten o'clock he finally returned to his room and had to rush to do at least some of his homework before he went to sleep.

What could Jack have done to improve his studying that night?

_____

_____

_____

3. Tony figured out that he had more than two hours of homework. He knew he'd go crazy if he had to sit still for that long and read and write. He decided to work out a schedule for himself. He would work for half an hour and then relax for 10 minutes. To relax he'd listen to music or talk with someone or something. Then he'd start working again. And he'd keep up that schedule until he had finished his homework.

What could Tony have done to improve his studying that night?

_____

_____

_____

SUMMARY

Concentration during a learning activity is not something that just happens. Rather, it must be intentional and strategic. And, like many other behaviors related to success, concentration must be practiced and will require self-discipline. When distracters are apparent, students must work to eliminate them quickly to avoid wasting academic time on something that is not productive.

- When hungry, eat.

- When tired, sleep.

- When sick, wait until the illness has passed.

- When a personal problem distracts, write it down in a brief note with the intent of dealing with it at a later time.

- When not interested in the topic, speak with the teacher about why learning the information is important.

TECHNOLOGY ADAPTATION

- Create a class blog for the purpose of electronically discussing the study skills tips—what works and what does not work.

USING YOUR TIME

ASSIGNMENT BEFORE CLASS

Directions: On the lines on the following page, write down everything that you do during the course of one average school day. Also, write the time of day of each activity and how much time you give to each activity. See the "Sample Record of a School Day" for an example of how to do this.

Keep track of the following:

1. The time of day that you began the activity

2. The type of activity

3. The amount of time given to each activity

RECORD OF A SCHOOL DAY

Date _____ Day of the Week _____

TIME OF DAY	ACTIVITY	LENGTH OF TIME

RECORD OF A SCHOOL DAY

Date _____ Day of the Week _____

TIME OF DAY	ACTIVITY	LENGTH OF TIME

RECORD OF A SCHOOL DAY

Date _____   Day of the Week _____

TIME OF DAY	ACTIVITY	LENGTH OF TIME

LEARNING FROM YOUR RECORD OF A SCHOOL DAY

Directions: Answer the questions below.

1. Examine your "Record" to find out how much time you gave to each of the kinds of activities listed below. Write the amount of time given to each kind of activity on the space to the right of that activity.

In School _____   Jobs _____   Homework _____

Activities _____   Sports _____   TV _____

Being with Friends _____   On the Phone _____

Meals _____   Relaxing/Free Time _____

Other _____

2. Looking at your record, do you see any use of time that surprises you? Do you see any use of time that you would like to change? If so, what?

_____

_____

_____

_____

SAMPLE RECORD OF A SCHOOL DAY

TIME OF DAY	ACTIVITY	LENGTH OF TIME
7:15 AM	Wake up	
7:20	Breakfast, get ready for school	40 minutes
8:00	Walk to school	30 minutes
8:30	In school	6 hours, 30 minutes
3:00 PM	Club/sports practice at school	1 hour
4:00	Talk to friends/hang out	30 minutes
4:30	Walk home	30 minutes

5:00	Listen to music/text on phone	1 hour, 10 minutes
6:10	Clean room/other chores	20 minutes
6:30	Dinner	40 minutes
7:10	Do dishes	20 minutes
7:30	Do homework	1 hour, 15 minutes
8:45	Surf Internet/watch TV	1 hour, 30 minutes
10:15	Get ready for next day/misc.	45 minutes
11:00	Go to sleep	

INTRODUCTION

One useful learning skill that can help you as much as any other is learning how to use your time well. A method that many people use to organize the way they use their time is a schedule. A schedule is a plan that you create for how you want to spend your time. First, you figure out what you need and want to do. Then you give a certain amount of time in your schedule to each activity.

A good schedule that you have created for yourself can help you avoid wasting time or getting behind in your schoolwork. It can help you make sure that you do what you must but also have time for what you want to do.

In this unit, you will learn about two kinds of schedules: a *daily schedule* and a *weekly schedule*.

WHAT SHOULD YOU KEEP IN MIND WHEN YOU ARE CREATING A SCHEDULE?

1. Try to make each day a "balanced" one. Give yourself time each day for work and play. Include time for schoolwork and chores at home, and for relaxation, exercise, and being with friends.

2. One part of your learning style is the time of day when you are most awake and alert. When you are most awake and alert, you can learn more efficiently. Figure out when you are most awake and alert, and make this your regular study time. Try to do your studying at this same time every day.

3. Try to spend at least some time during every school day doing schoolwork. If you have no homework due the next day, use your regular study time for long-term assignments or reading. Make studying during your regular study time a habit. The more you get used to doing schoolwork at that time, the easier it will be for you to study then.

4. Be sure to give yourself some free time each day. People need unplanned time to relax and unwind.

CREATING A DAILY SCHEDULE

In this exercise, you are going to create a *daily schedule* for the next school day. First, read over the directions carefully that follow in the next section. Then, look at the example of daily schedules on the following pages. Now, go back to direction #1 below, and, using the blank schedule on the following pages, start to make your *daily schedule* for the next school day. Follow directions #1–6.

Be sure to write your schedule in pencil, so you can change it if you need to do so. When you have finished your schedule and are satisfied with it, you can write it over in pen if you like.

You may also choose to keep an electronic planner using an app from the Internet for your smart phone, tablet device, or computer. There are many planning software applications available with various styles to meet the needs of the individual user.

Directions:

1. Write the day of the week that is your next school day in the space provided on the schedule form.

2. Mark down the time you will wake up on this day, and when you will go to sleep. Then mark down the time you will spend eating meals and being in school.

3. Next, write down your obligations—things you must do for the day you are planning. For example: part-time job, religious school, taking care of siblings, practices, and so forth.

4. Now, fill in your study time(s). Pick the time(s) when you are most alert. Be sure to give yourself enough time to get your schoolwork done well.

5. Look at the time you have left, and fill it in with other activities. Be sure to give yourself some time for things you enjoy. Also, leave yourself enough free, unplanned time.

6. Now, look at your schedule carefully. How does it seem to you? If it seems reasonable and helpful, you are finished. If not, change it so you are comfortable with it.

UNIT XII

DAILY SCHEDULE

Day 1: _____

6:00 AM	
7:00	
8:00	
9:00	
10:00	
11:00	
12:00 PM	
1:00	
2:00	
3:00	
4:00	
5:00	
6:00	
7:00	
8:00	
9:00	
10:00	
11:00	

DAILY SCHEDULE EXAMPLE

6:00 AM	
7:00	(7:15) Wake up; (7:20) Breakfast/get ready
8:00	(8:00) Walk to school (8:30) In school
9:00	
10:00	
11:00	
12:00 PM	
1:00	
2:00	
3:00	(3:00) Club/sports practice at school
4:00	(4:00) Talk with friends/hang out (4:30) Walk home
5:00	(5:00) Listen to music/text on phone
6:00	(6:10) Clean room/other chores (6:30) Dinner
7:00	(7:10) Do dishes (7:30) Do homework
8:00	(8:45) Surf Internet/watch TV
9:00	
10:00	(10:15) Get ready for next day/misc.
11:00	(11:00) Go to sleep

USING YOUR SCHEDULE: WHAT HAPPENED?

You now have a schedule that you have created for yourself. The next step is up to you. Try to follow your schedule for that day.

At the end of the day, take a few minutes to answer the questions below about how well your schedule worked for you.

1. How much did you follow your schedule? Circle the word or words below that best describe how much you followed your schedule.

    completely   mostly   some   a little   not at all

2. If you followed all or most of your schedule, how did you feel about using it?

    _____

    _____

3. If you didn't follow much of your schedule, what got in the way of your using it?

    _____

    _____

4. How useful did you find your schedule?

    _____

    _____

5. Do you think you will try creating another schedule? Why or why not?

    _____

    _____

CREATING A WEEKLY SCHEDULE

Some people find a daily schedule very helpful. Others find it too much trouble to be worth the effort. For some people, a *weekly schedule* can be of more value than a daily schedule. Furthermore, using an electronic planner is an easy way to integrate all scheduling activities. Electronic planners can be simply a calendar on a digital device, eliminating the need for a paper calendar. Alternatively, an electronic planner can be more robust and be fully integrated between a user's mobile device (smart phone, tablet, or computer), e-mail, or other digital device, and allow the user to be fully connected and in sync with an updated calendar at all times. Electronic planners allow for automatic reminders of appointments and tasks and allow for input of these tasks and appointments from multiple sources.

One way to create a *weekly schedule* is to make a daily schedule for each day and put them all together. You can find printed schedule books that have a page or space for each day in most office supply stores. Usually these schedule books include all the days in a year, with the days in each week grouped together.

Another way to make a *weekly schedule* is to list on the schedule only those events or obligations that are not part of your usual routine. When you make this kind of schedule, you assume that you already know about the things you do every day, for example, eating meals, helping at home, going to school, and so forth. You use the schedule to help you plan and remember special events and responsibilities, for example, studying for tests, parties, doing long-range projects, and so forth. You can look at an example of this kind of weekly schedule in the next section. Students may experiment using the space provided.

If you want to experiment with this kind of weekly schedule, use the schedule form provided. When you have followed it for a week, answer the questions about "using your schedule" to see how it worked for you.

USING A SCHEDULE: A FEW LAST WORDS

Some people like using schedules. Others do not. Some people can benefit from writing out a schedule and following it. Other people may already plan this way in their heads.

When you consider using a schedule, the key question is this: Can making and using a schedule help you do what you want and need to do? If it can, then use it. If not, then do not.

When you use a schedule, remember that it is a tool to help you, not to control you. Be flexible with it. Follow your schedule as much as you can, but recognize that you may need to change it at times.

WEEKLY SCHEDULE

	Day 1 Sunday	Day 2 Monday	Day 3 Tuesday	Day 4 Wednesday	Day 5 Thursday	Day 6 Friday	Day 7 Saturday
Morning		Math test					Soccer game!
Early Afternoon						English paper due	
Late Afternoon				Help around the house	Rewrite English paper		
Evening	Study for math test					Chris's party	

WEEKLY SCHEDULE

	Day 1 Sunday	Day 2 Monday	Day 3 Tuesday	Day 4 Wednesday	Day 5 Thursday	Day 6 Friday	Day 7 Saturday
Morning							
Early Afternoon							
Late Afternoon							
Evening							

SUMMARY

- A schedule is a plan that you create for how you want to spend your time.

- A good schedule can help you do both what you <u>must do</u> and what you <u>want to do</u>.

- When you make a schedule for yourself, keep the following ideas in mind:

  o Try to make each day a "balanced" one, giving yourself time for both work and play.

  o Figure out when you are most awake and alert, and try to do your studying then.

  o Try to spend at least some time during each school day studying. If you have no homework due the next day, work on long-term projects.

- One kind of schedule is a *daily schedule*. Another kind is a *weekly schedule*.

- Scheduling can be kept using a paper planner from an office supply store or using an electronic planner (daily or weekly). The electronic planner can be simply a calendar on a digital device, eliminating the need for a paper calendar. An electronic planner can be more robust and be fully integrated between a user's mobile device (smart phone, tablet, or computer), e-mail, or other digital device, and allow the user to be fully connected and in sync with an updated calendar at all times.

- The purpose of any schedule that you make for yourself is to help you organize your time better, so you can do what you want and need to do.

- Keep a schedule using a digital device can be fun. Using an electronic planner to keep track of your time versus a traditional planner allows you to access it anywhere you have Internet access without having to carry a paper version with you. In most cases, you can access your preferred planner using your smart phone or tablet.

- In addition to keeping track of time, online planners allow you to organize and keep track of your assignments. You can easily track when projects are due and keep track of your grades for each class. If your schedule becomes too intense, you can easily modify and make adjustments. Some online planners will chart your daily, weekly, and monthly activities and summarize where you are choosing to spend your time and how much time you are spending on each part of your schedule.

- Online planners can be personalized to meet the needs of users. You can choose backgrounds and color styles, and add graphics in some cases. Making something more appealing makes you more likely to use it.

TECHNOLOGY ADAPTATION

- Using the Internet, research various online devices for assisting with time management. Make a listing of the ones you believe would be most beneficial to you as a student.